HAUNTED
HAMPSHIRE

T0294489

HAUNTED
HAMPSHIRE

RUPERT MATTHEWS

The
History
Press

First published 2009
Reprinted 2016

The History Press
The Mill, Brimscombe Port
Stroud, Gloucestershire, GL5 2QG
www.thehistorypress.co.uk

British Library Cataloguing in Publication Data.
A catalogue record for this book is available from the British Library.

ISBN 978 0 7524 4862 6

Typesetting and origination by The History Press

CONTENTS

INTRODUCTION

There are few counties in England more varied or more beautiful than Hampshire.

The scenery is as splendid as anyone could wish. In the north are the chalk uplands and heaths that mark the northern edge of the coastal counties from Kent to Dorset. From these uplands tumble down crystal clear streams such as the Itchen and Test that are the finest trout streams in Britain. Together they create the riverside scenery so typical of the central part of the county.

The county city of Winchester is certainly of Roman date, and probably much earlier, though firm archaeological evidence is lacking. Around the year 490 it was home to a Romano-British nobleman named Cerdic. This Cerdic was the local governor of the Belgae territory who declared himself independent of the crumbling institutions of post-Roman Britain, and hired a band of English mercenaries to secure himself in power. He thus not only played his part in undermining post-Roman Britain, but also founded the dynastic line that would later become known as the House of Cerdic, giving rise to the royal family of Wessex and through them lead to our present monarch.

The coastal strip of the county has long been dominated by the great ports of Southampton and Portsmouth, though in more recent years the holiday and retirement homes that have always been prominent on Hayling Island and the Witterings have spread out to overlook the beaches and inlets that alternately make up the Hampshire coast. The New Forest has been – quite literally – a law unto itself ever since the area was turned into forest by the Norman Kings for their hunting pleasures. Special forest laws held sway here, enforced by separate courts.

The ghosts and phantoms of Hampshire are no less varied than the landscape they inhabit. There are spectres of the rich and famous to be encountered – Florence Nightingale and King William II among them – but there are also the wraiths of penniless peddlers and struggling workmen to be met. Some of Hampshire's ghosts are inoffensive and retiring. Others are undeniably scary, and even terrifying. Most seem to be going about the county on business of their own without taking any notice of we mere mortals, who glimpse them from time to time. And there is no shortage of these supernatural inhabitants. On my travels around this charming county it sometimes seemed that I could barely move for ghosts. More than once, I pulled up in a village to investigate some ghost or other only to find that other spectres and phantoms had their haunts there.

I must thank the people of Hampshire, both for their help in putting this book together, and for their unfailing courtesy toward a traveller in search of spooks and ghosts. Some have been happy for me to quote them talking about their experiences, and I thank them for that. Others have preferred to remain anonymous, which is fair enough and I have respected their choice.

I will close with a simple observation. It is all very well reading about ghosts and spectres, but there is nothing to compare with actually getting out and visiting the haunted site itself. Even when the ghost does not put in an appearance, there is some intangible and yet very real atmosphere to these places that can be fully appreciated only during a visit. I would urge all readers to go out on the road to investigate these haunted places for themselves.

With a county as charming and welcoming as Hampshire, it would be an effort amply rewarded.

THE NORTH

The little town of Odiham stands just south of junction five of the M3, where the A287 meets the motorway, and it is very possibly the oldest in the county. Long before either 'M' or 'A' roads were thought of, the prehistoric trade track known today as the Harrow Way ran here. Archaeological digs have shown that people lived here when Rome was a group of mud huts on a bare hillside and Athens a huddle of hovels. The vast chalk pit just south of the town was being worked from about 1200 B.C. It was prized flint and greenstone that was traded along the Harrow Way, along with more perishable leather, livestock and cloth.

The High Street is among the widest in England, and its width is the first thing to strike a visitor. The roadway was made like this to allow a stagecoach pulled by a team of four horses to turn around, the coaching trade between London and the ports of the south coast being a major industry from medieval times until the coming of the railways. The George Hotel was the most luxurious and prestigious of the inns that catered to the coach trade. The oldest parts of the building date back to 1540, though most of what stands today dates back to a major rebuilding that took place in the mid-eighteenth century. So does the ghost.

As ghosts go, the one that lurks here is pretty scary. Fortunately, it is most unlikely you will encounter anything more frightening these days than a particularly well-cooked bit of seafood, but that is for later.

About 250 years ago, which is when the story of the haunting begins, the area around Odiham was not a particularly pleasant place to loiter. The village was nice enough, but the countryside around was the hunting ground of highwaymen, footpads and violent robbers of all kinds. By that date the hotel had already had a colourful history. It had played host to many important dignitaries on their way to London from the south-west. It also doubled up as the courthouse on occasion, and was even the chosen home of wealthier French prisoners during the long wars of the eighteenth century.

In those days, the George catered for the local gentry. Mindful of the unsavoury nature of the surrounding roads at night, The George kept a coach to hand to take its esteemed guests home if they stayed late and became rather the worse for wear. The coachman who ferried his merry customers home prudently kept a pistol under his seat in case he encountered a man of evil intent.

His new young wife, however, worried about him. Each night she waited in their room at the rear of the hotel anxiously listening out for the hoof-beats that told her that her husband was safely home.

One particular night she heard the longed for hoof-beats and dashed to her door to welcome her husband. Opening the door, the poor woman was struck dumb with fright. There was no coach and no husband. Just a lone figure standing in the yard. The figure was a woman in a long grey cloak, but it was the figure's face that held the attention. It was a great terrifying emptiness. There was simply nothing there – yet it managed to be ugly and filled with hate and evil. As the wife watched aghast, the hideous figure stared at her for seconds which seemed like hours. Then the spectral woman turned and drifted across the yard, disappearing into the shadows at the far end.

Moments later, the coach pulled into the yard, the coachman safe and well. Despite this, the man's wife took the apparition to be a clear warning to quit the job at once. After some

The George Hotel in Odiham; the scene of a gruesome haunting in the past, and a fine fish restaurant in the present.

persuasion, her husband gave up his risky, if lucrative, duties and went to work at another inn where he was given employment safely behind the bar.

The hideous old hag has not been seen recently. Sarah, the receptionist, greeted me warmly when I called. She happily showed me round to the stable yard where the ghost lurked. It is now a cheery, open space which has lost whatever sinister atmosphere it might once have had. Tables protected by large sun shades are scattered about the yard, each with its complement of chairs, though there were no drinkers when I called as the weather was a bit nippy and a chilly wind whipped autumnal leaves around the place.

Inside was another story. I looked around the warmly comfortable restaurant as I contemplated the dessert menu. I could not imagine why the ghost had not returned since a refurbishment some ten years back. With lunch over, it was time to investigate reports of ghosts out at Odiham Castle. The ruined fortress stands a mile or so west of the town just off the towpath of the old Basingstoke Canal. By the time I had finished lunch the wind had dropped and a bright autumn sun had come out. Nevertheless, there was something brooding about the ruins of Odiham Castle. The atmosphere was decidedly odd.

The day was chilly and dry, but around the castle the air was damp, almost clammy. The tall, overhanging trees cut out much of the sun and blocked any sounds from distant roads. The only noise was that of the fallen leaves rustling and tumbling over the ground in the breeze.

No doubt the strangeness of the place is enhanced by the fact that it is difficult to find, for there are no signs to guide the visitor to these tumbled ruins. You could walk to the castle from Odiham, but it is a bit of a stretch and might take you an hour each way. I would recommend that you drive. Either way, leave Odiham village and get on to the B3349 heading north. At a small roundabout, turn left down the road towards Upton Grey. Almost at once there is a narrow road on your right which carries no signpost at all, but it does warn drivers that there is a ford which is unsuitable for motor vehicles. There is, indeed, and this is where you should

The stable yard of the George Hotel in Odiham. It was here that the phantom materialised.

A ruined tower at Odiham Castle. In its heyday 700 years ago, Odiham was as much a royal residence as a fortified castle. The living quarters were sumptuous.

A sketch of the phantom guard of Odiham Castle, as based on an eyewitness account.

The doorway leading to the dungeons at Odiham Castle.

park your car. Follow the footpath to the left just beside the ford. This path takes you across a field and through a gate to emerge on the banks of the canal. Turn right along the towpath. The castle is about 100 yards on your right.

Once you eventually get there, there is only a forlorn notice erected by the council giving information on the place. This is how ruins used to be, overgrown with weeds and neglected by the hand of authority. These are no tidy heritage-style ruins which have been all spruced up and made safe. They are falling-down ruins. It is as if the castle's owners just got up and went away one day. Since then nature and the wild wood have had the place to themselves.

The site has definite atmosphere. But does it have a ghost? If so, who is it and is there more than one?

An old book that I found in the archives of the British Library was in no doubt about the local spectre. 'The ghost', it declared confidently, 'is that of a minstrel boy from times long past. The youth's charming pipes can be heard drifting romantically through the ruins. The beauty and charm of the haunting need no emphasis for this tumbling ruin is the perfect backdrop to such a phantom musician.'

Someone of more practical opinions had obviously been to the ruins since then. It is now plastered with signs loudly proclaiming 'DANGER' and warning of falling masonry and loose stones. Any romance or beauty was clearly lost on the council engineer.

A man was walking his dog along the towpath when I called. Had he heard the phantom minstrel?

'Ah, well. No', the man said as his large dog bounded around like a puppy. 'Not me. But there is a ghost here, no doubt about it. Bloke in a helmet. They do say that King John was here before he went off up to Windsor to sign Magna Carta, see. And a right foul mood he was in too. Perhaps he's here still.' Perhaps.

I got more detailed information from a lady named Vanessa, who lives in North Warnborough. She told me a more detailed story:

Way back in the middle ages the English captured David, King of Scotland. They wanted to hold him to ransom, as was the custom back then when you had an important prisoner. And they needed to hold him in a secure place a long way from Scotland. They chose Odiham Castle. It had been built to be a fortified home by King John so it had comfortable rooms for the Scottish King as well as being surrounded by thick stone walls. Obviously the King of Scotland was none too pleased to be held prisoner, but he had plenty of money and was allowed to buy in various luxuries. One of the things he paid for was a minstrel. The young lad would soothe the imprisoned King with his pipe music. And that is what the haunting is all about. The pipe music is the King's minstrel. The ghosts people see are the guards who kept the King of Scotland imprisoned.

Vanessa gave me a brief description of these phantom men. I made a sketch from her description.

Not far south of Odiham is the little village of Well, with the Chequers pub at its heart. This charming fifteenth-century structure has a distinctive olde-worlde atmosphere to it with wooden beams and open log fires, giving a warm and welcoming greeting to the large numbers of regular customers. A former barmaid here told me that 'people are always seeing things', but quite what the things were that they were always seeing she was not entirely certain.

Fortunately, I managed to get hold of the new landlord as I was writing this book. He responded to an email, writing:

I have been here two years, and have to say that during the early part of my tenure, strange things did happen here.

The ghost is reputed to be that of a landlady, who apparently was murdered in the cellar area of the pub. She is thought to be fond of one corner of the seated area of the bar area – and when I took over I used to push a table right into the corner where she liked to sit. In the night, I could hear furniture being moved and when I went down to investigate, would find the table I had pushed hard into the corner, moved out by about two foot!

Another odd occurrence was that the hot water tap in the gents loo was being turned on full during the night, even though I had made sure it was turned off securely before retiring.

This activity seemed to stop shortly after my black cat arrived at the premises – or maybe she [the ghost] doesn't see me as a threat anymore!

The Crown and Cushion on the road from Minley to Blackwater is a friendly public house with a menu to tempt anyone. It was not always thus. Back in 1671, this was a private house that was being rented by an Irish soldier by the name of Colonel Thomas Blood, though at this stage in his life he was using the name Thomas Ayloffe. He had already led a fairly colourful life by the time he came to live in Hampshire under an assumed name.

Blood was born the son of an Irish blacksmith who had risen to become so prosperous that he had become an MP and rented a castle as his home in County Meath. When the English Civil War broke out in 1642, the twenty-four year old Blood picked up his sword and rode

CHARLES II.

King Charles II was instrumental, albeit unwittingly, in causing the haunting at Minley.

off to join the King's forces. After a couple of years, however, Blood switched his allegiance to Parliament and ended the war as a trusted officer in Oliver Cromwell's own cavalry regiment. Blood was rewarded with estates confiscated from Royalists and retired to Ireland with the assumed title of colonel (in fact, he had never reached a rank higher than captain).

When Cromwell died and King Charles II ascended to the throne, Blood found that most of his profitable estates were confiscated and returned to their original owners. In 1663, Blood joined a conspiracy of ex-Parliamentarians in Ireland that aimed to overthrow the new government, proclaim Ireland a republic and make Catholicism the official religion. Blood's part in the plot was to storm Dublin Castle and to kidnap or kill the Duke of Ormonde, the Lord Lieutenant of Ireland.

The day before Blood was due to strike, the plot was betrayed to Ormonde who ordered the arrest of the conspirators. Blood managed to fight his way past those sent to arrest him and, after some weeks on the run, found a ship willing to take him to France. The other conspirators were not so lucky, being strung up by Ormonde on the walls of Dublin Castle without trial. When Blood heard the news, he swore vengeance against Ormonde.

After serving as a mercenary in the Dutch army for several years, Blood made contact with the Duke of Buckingham. This Buckingham was a massively wealthy and utterly dissolute nobleman who was a great friend of King Charles II. More importantly, he had been ousted from a number of positions by the same Ormonde who was so hated by Blood. Using money and contacts provided by Buckingham, Blood adopted the name of Ayloffe, set himself up as an apothecary and moved to Hampshire. He brought with him his 'wife', actually a mistress named Cushenor Cussens.

From Hampshire, Ayloffe made contact with a number of London criminals and disaffected Irishmen and concocted a plot to kill Ormonde, who was now living in London. Exactly how deeply Buckingham was involved is unclear, but on the night of 6 December 1670 the conspirators struck. Ormonde's coach was halted by a gang of masked men in St James's Street. Ormonde was

Cromwell's cavalry prepare to charge at the Battle of Naseby. Colonel Blood was serving as a captain in this regiment at Naseby, before he was forced to change his name and live in hiding at Minley.

dragged out, tied to a horse and led toward Tyburn (now Marble Arch), the traditional site for the execution of criminals. Just as Blood and his men were about to string up the unfortunate Ormonde, one of Ormonde's servants rode up firing pistols and hacking about him with a sword. In the confusion Ormonde got away.

Meanwhile, Blood had been inveigling his way into the company of various people. Among these was Talbot Edwards, the keeper of the crown jewels in the Tower of London. Blood, posing as Parson Burke, met Edwards apparently by accident and spent several weeks getting to know him and his family. Edwards had an unmarried daughter, and Blood then invented an imaginary and wealthy Irish nephew who was looking for an English wife with good connections. Tempted by the tales of Irish lands, Edwards invited Blood and members of his family to come to the Tower of London to view the Crown Jewels. The fateful visit was set for 9 May 1671.

Blood turned up at Edwards's quarters in the Tower with three relatives who were all, like him, armed to the teeth. As soon as Edwards let them in, Blood and his gang drew their weapons. Edwards, his wife and daughter were quickly overpowered and trussed up. Blood grabbed the crown, hammering it flat to fit under his parson's robes, while the gang tucked the rest of the regalia into pockets and bags. They then slipped out the door.

To Blood's astonishment, Edwards's son, Whythe, was at that moment arriving home instead of being with his regiment in Flanders as he was supposed to be. Sensing something was wrong, he challenged 'Parson Burke', who promptly whipped out a pistol and opened fire – but missed. The shot brought the guards running, arriving as Blood and his gang were spurring their horses out of the main gate toward a fishing boat hired for a quick escape by sea. The guards were scattered, but a quick-thinking Captain Beckman, who was drilling a squad outside the walls, led his men to the attack and blocked the route to the wharf. Blood's accomplices surrendered, but Blood threw the battered crown at Beckman and drew his sword. He gave up only after being severely wounded.

Hauled off to prison, 'Parson Burke' was quickly identified as Colonel Thomas Blood. He was put on trial not only for the attempted theft of the crown jewels, but also for the attempted murder of Ormonde and for high treason for his part in the Irish plot of 1663. Blood refused to talk to anybody, declaring that since his crime had been to try to steal the crown he would answer to nobody but the King himself. At his trial he said nothing and was condemned to death.

News spread rapidly that the notorious Colonel Blood had been captured at long last, and that his prompt execution was expected to take place almost at once. When word reached Minley, 'Mrs Ayloffe', supposedly the apothecary's wife, fainted dead away. When she came to, the poor woman was clearly half-mad and deeply distressed. Not knowing the cause of her upset, friends took her home to what is now the Crown and Cushion.

For days she did nothing but wander around the house and gardens wringing her hands and sobbing. Every time a rider or carriage came past, she would run out into the road demanding if there were any news from London. There was always plenty of news, but never anything that she wanted to hear. A few days later she died. The rumour was that she had committed suicide by drowning herself in a nearby pond, though officially she was said to have died of apoplexy – then a term commonly used when a doctor was either uncertain of a cause or unwilling to declare it publicly.

Meanwhile, King Charles II had been listening to reports about Blood and his various activities. Having himself been a wanted man and forced to live on the run after the Royalist defeat in the Civil War, Charles seems to have recognised something of himself in Blood. He agreed to meet Blood before the execution. Blood was dragged into the palace and hustled, securely bound, into the presence of King Charles, who had with him not only Buckingham and Ormonde but also Prince Rupert, who had commanded the Royalist cavalry in the Civil War, then turned pirate and sailed the High Seas for a while after the conflict.

Asked if he had anything to say to excuse his crimes, Blood smiled and replied that he had none: 'It was a gallant attempt, but unsuccessful.' King Charles then asked, 'How now, knave. What if I should give you your life?' Blood bowed deeply and replied, 'Then I would endeavour to deserve it, Sire!' Charles laughed. He ordered that Blood be set free and given estates to recompense him for those lost in 1662. Ormonde was furious, so Charles added the rider that the death sentence on Blood still stood and would be put into effect if he committed even the slightest crime.

Blood spent the rest of his life quietly, dividing his time between his new lands in Ireland and London. He died in the capital on 23 August 1680 and was buried in St Margaret's Churchyard, now Christchurch Gardens. After his funeral it was discovered that he had debts of over £10,000. The men to whom he owed money demanded that the body be exhumed and shown to them as they suspected he had faked his death to escape the debt. He hadn't – the body was his and was reburied. Buckingham paid for a headstone on condition that it carried the lines that he had written about Blood:

> He lies the man who boldly hath run though
> More villainies than England ever knew;
> and ne'er to any friend he had was true.
> Here let him then by all unpitied lie,
> And let's rejoice his time was come to die

Which seems a bit harsh. Blood's son, Holcroft Blood, rose to be a distinguished military officer and commanded the British artillery at the Battle of Blenheim in 1704.

Meanwhile, the good folk of Minley had discovered just who their friendly and jovial apothecary Ayloffe had really been, and why his wife had reacted so violently to the news of Blood's arrest. Not only that, but her ghost began to be seen just outside her old home. She was seen to be weeping, wringing her hands and watching the road anxiously for riders and travellers coming from London.

It is said that her ghost is seen there still. She takes the form of a tall lady wearing a long grey gown, and with her hair worn long and tumbling down her back. The man who told me of this sad spectre said that he had seen her when driving home from a friend's house one evening:

> I had not been drinking or anything. I was driving along around 9pm with my mind on a problem at work. Then suddenly there she was. Just sort of standing by the side of the road. She was all grey and a bit misty-like as my headlights swept over her. At first I thought she was just a woman walking by the road. But then she wasn't there. It was odd. I can't say that I actually saw her vanish – not like a ghost does in films anyhow. She was there, then she wasn't.

The building, which dates back to 1512, became an inn soon afterward. It took its unusual name from the crown that Blood had tried to steal and the name of his 'wife', Cushenor. Next door to the pub stands a medieval feasting hall which, rather unusually, did not stand there in Blood's day. It was transported in pieces from Wiltshire in the 1970s when it was threatened with demolition. The barn was re-erected here to serve as a function room, complete with all modern facilities.

Another pub with royal connections and a rather insubstantial phantom lady is Andover's White Hart in Bridge Street. The inn was built back in 1617 and, unlike the Crown and

Cushion, it was built to be a tavern and stopping place for travellers. Its more illustrious guests in the past have included King Charles I. The pub now has twenty-two comfortable en-suite rooms, which some claim would satisfy even the current monarch!

It is one of those rooms, and the corridor outside, that is said to be the favoured haunt of the Green Lady. Room twenty is as convivial as any visitor could expect, and the ghost is no trouble. She is seen sometimes, standing by the window or walking down the corridor in a long green dress. She stays in sight for only a second or two before she vanishes. Who she was in life and why she returns are total mysteries.

Rather more solid are the ghosts of the White Hart on London Road in Basingstoke. Seen so often are these phantoms that they have been the subject of a lengthy investigation by patron and paranormal investigator Jim Bridgeman and the In Search of Proof paranormal investigation team.

The main phantom is that of a tall man who walks into an upstairs bedroom, smooths his hair and then leaves again. This phantom was reported soon after the war, and continues to be seen at intervals right up to the present day. The most recent detailed report I have is from 2007, but sightings have continued. This gentleman seems to be fairly content with his lot and is no bother to anyone.

Occurring almost as often is the phantom of Little Jack, said to have been a young boy who was hung in what would have been the courtyard of the pub, now the beer garden, for stealing alcohol. He has never been seen but rather his presence has often been felt. At some points his presence has been felt enough to cause people to cry at the overwhelming pathos of the incident. During paranormal investigations, the first question asked by almost any medium or sensitive is, 'Who is Jack?'

Jim himself has seen the third ghost, that of the 'well-dressed gentleman'. Jim says:

> I have been witness to this spirit on one occasion. Mediums feel he was a local watch maker that spent a lot of time at the pub. He has been seen sat alone at empty tables and walking around. When people have done a double-take thinking 'who the hell is this character' he is nowhere to be seen. On the occasion I saw him it was as if I physically bumped into him. I was stood near the bar talking to a few friends and I felt someone bump into me, as happens when the bar is busy, and out of the corner of my eye I saw someone in period dress which confused me. So I turned around to say 'sorry mate' as you do but no one was there and the bar behind me had only two people in it who were sat down. This one baffles me to this day.

Jim has also seen the phantom dog:

> A ghost dog has been seen and felt at the pub; I had also witnessed this occurrence. I saw a dog run through the pub from one bar to the next. Knowing dogs weren't allowed in the pub I got up to find out whose dog it was and take it outside. On getting to the top bar there was no dog and the door was closed.

The full story of these hauntings can be read on the In Search of Proof website at: www.insearchofproof.co.uk/locations/white_hart/white_hart_vid.WMV

As its name might suggest, the Poplar Farm Inn at Abbots Ann, north of Andover, was built as a farm, and remained as such until fairly recently. Sometime during the eighteenth century, local legend has it that the farm was bought by a grand lady from London. The lady paid cash and behaved in a most unusual manner. The farm's land was rented out to nearby farmers and the house itself completely redecorated – the decorators again being paid in cash. Paying in cash was very unusual behaviour for gentry in those days. It was far more usual for bills to be settled at the so-called 'quarter-days', of which there were four each year.

Once the house was completed to the lady's satisfaction, she hired a mere skeleton staff. There was a housekeeper, a housemaid and a couple of gardeners. Otherwise the place was left empty for several weeks. Then a messenger came from London carrying written instructions of great detail accompanied by a bulging purse to pay for any bills incurred. The housekeeper was instructed to lay in vast quantities of wine, food and provisions, but all food was to be already cooked and prepared before being laid out in the kitchen for inspection. The beds were to be made with freshly laundered linen and all the crockery and cutlery be got out and cleaned thoroughly. The stables were to be stocked with hay and straw ready for several horses to be stabled. In short, the house was to be prepared for a visit by the lady and some friends.

The most astonishing part of the instructions were left to last. Once everything was ready, the staff were to leave the house unlocked and go home. They were not to return for any reason at all for seven days. On the seventh day, they were to return to clean the house and put everything back into storage.

When the day came for the house to receive its guests, the staff got everything ready and then went home as instructed. Of course, word of the odd orders had got about. The villagers watched with curiosity as a number of carriages rumbled to the village, deposited their passengers and then departed. One gentlemen dressed in costly clothes of the latest fashion arrived on horseback. The guests entered the house, and nothing more was seen of them. Lights burned brightly from the windows at night and the strains of music drifted out but neither the grand lady nor her guests were seen out and about. On the seventh day the guests departed as mysteriously as they had arrived.

The housekeeper, maid and gardeners trooped back to the house and were astonished at what they found. The place was a wreck. The wine and food had been consumed in what had obviously been a debauched orgy of the utmost depravity. Plates and furniture were wrecked, the beds showed signs of energetic activity while the gardens had been turned up by boots and hooves engaged in goodness knew what. On the hall table was a purse of gold coins with a handwritten note from the lady herself, instructing the staff to clear up the mess, replace damages and await further orders. Muttering and gossiping the staff did as instructed.

A few months later, once again there came written orders from London accompanied by a purse of gold coins. The staff was ordered to prepare the house for a visit by a number of people and stock it with prodigious amounts of food and drink before making themselves scarce. This time the villagers inspected the arriving guests with rather more interest, but other than the fact that they were clearly rich and well dressed there was no clue to their identities. Once again the house was left a mess by the drunken debauchery that took place.

For several years the process was repeated. Then word came that the mysterious lady had died and that her heirs no longer needed the farm, which was put up for sale. It stayed a farm until the mid-twentieth century, after which it was a private house for some years, eventually becoming a pub in the 1970s.

And through all that time the phantom of a lady in a long, dark dress of heavy silk was seen walking up and down the main staircase. Doors opened and closed by themselves, footsteps echoed from empty rooms. It was, of course, widely believed that the phantom 'Lady in Black' was the wraith of the mysterious lady who had led the wild, drunken orgies in the eighteenth century. Certainly no other figure in the history of the building had a life as colourful, nor any likely reason to return in spectral form.

Whether the Lady in Black is coming back to relive her days of debauched revels or to atone for them nobody can know.

The highwayman Captain Jacques came to a sticky end and now haunts The Royal Anchor at Liphook.

A very different type of lady might be behind the haunting of the Greyfriar pub at Chawton. The pub stands opposite the charming house in which the great novelist Jane Austen lived from 1805 to 1817. She completed seven of her novels here and the place is now preserved as a museum to her memory. She wrote of it soon after moving in:

> Our Chawton Home, how much we find
> Already in it to our mind
> And now convinced, that when complete
> It will all other houses best
> That ever have been made or mended
> With rooms concise or rooms distended.

Maybe not her greatest lines, I would suggest, but she clearly loved the place.

Perhaps inevitably Jane Austen has been identified as the spectre that is sometimes seen and sensed in the pub opposite. The ghost seemed to be active in the 1960s, but I have not been able to find any witnesses willing to state that they have seen or heard anything more recently. Personally, I cannot imagine why anyone would abandon this excellent pub.

Several other pub ghosts are similarly inclined not to be terribly active these days. The ghost of the Cricketers at Yateley is said to be that of a German spy arrested here in the Second World War and subsequently shot. He was, in years gone by, said to fiddle with glasses and electronic equipment, but not any longer, apparently.

The Royal Anchor at Liphook has a similarly inactive spook, though this one does at least have a name: Captain Jacques. This rather swashbuckling character was a highwayman who

Hook's White Hart sign hides a spectre of a boy in breeches who dates back to the pub's earliest days.

lurked on the lonely roads that ran across Longstone and Bosham marshes on the coast far to the south. At Liphook, Captain Jacques – he was (or claimed to be) French – made himself popular by spending freely. He bought drinks for local gentlemen and tipped the staff handsomely. He claimed to be a merchant, but more than one person suspected the truth.

Captain Jacques was staying in what is now room six when the forces of law and order caught up with him. Captain Jacques had chosen his bolthole well, as the room had a secret door next to the fireplace that led down to the stable yard. When the magistrate's men appeared, Captain Jacques decided to make a fight of it. He fired at them in the bar when they tried to arrest him, then raced up to his room. As he clearly hoped, the pursuers ran up after him only to find the door bolted from the inside. No doubt Captain Jacques hoped to get down to his horse in the stable by way of the secret stairway while his pursuers were in the corridor upstairs.

Things did not work out that way. One of the lawmen was a prodigiously strong giant of a man who booted the door of room six off its hinges with one mighty kick. Captain Jacques was caught scrabbling at the wall. In view of his willingness to open fire earlier, the attackers chose to shoot first and ask questions later. Captain Jacques was shot dead.

The secret stair was subsequently removed, but the ghost remained. Clad in a tricorn hat and dashing riding cloak, the ghostly highwayman was seen often lurking in the fatal room six. No longer, apparently. He seems to have passed on to wherever ghostly highwaymen go.

Hook's White Hart public house – Hampshire seems to have more than its fair share of inns with this name – lies on the A30 London Road in the centre of town. There is a car park beside the pub if you are visiting, or a large public car park opposite. Just for once it is not the pub itself that is said to be haunted, but the streets outside.

'Ah well. Now then,' began Keith, the landlord, when I called to investigate. 'I haven't actually seen him myself. Not as such. But there is a ghost here right enough.'

I took a good pull on my pint. I had actually come to Hook to look for a different ghost entirely, but more of that later. Now I was in the bar of the White Hart waiting for my lunch to arrive and found I had stumbled on to a second phantom in Hook. But what was it?

'It's a boy, about ten years old say. Something like that. He wears a pair of breeches, real old-fashioned.' It sounds as if this youngster was a servant back in the old days. Young lads were often employed to fetch and carry at old inns. They might help with the horses, serve ale to guests or help with the cleaning. These days, of course, child labour is frowned upon, but back then it was a natural part of everyday life. Back when, though? Judging by what witnesses have said about the boy he would seem to date from the seventeenth or eighteenth century.

That set me thinking about the other ghost in Hook. Judging by the fashions, the boy in the White Hart might date from about the same period. But what did Keith mean when he said he had not seen the phantom boy 'as such'?

It seems that although the ghostly boy is seen from time to time in the bar, Keith has not seen the phantom himself. Others have, though, and the description they give is clear enough. The boy does not restrict himself to just standing around or walking through doors. One of the pictures in the bar has a habit of moving. It is always going crooked, as if someone has moved it. Now I know of many such things, doors that slam and the like. Often it is the wind. But not here, apparently. People have seen it move. One minute it is as immobile as any other picture, the next it suddenly starts swinging from side to side. And the glass jar of cherries moves as well. Now this was more interesting. The jar in question is heavy and no draft or gust of wind could possibly shift it.

The White Hart is an old pub, dating back some centuries. The road on which it stands is the old London Road and was once one of the major coaching routes from London to the south-west of England. The White Hart catered for the passing trade and the boy in breeches would, no doubt, have been familiar to the travellers.

So what of the other ghost, the one that brought me to Hook in the first place? That is the phantom of a cavalier who lurks at night in the streets around Station Road. At least, he used to lurk there. More than one old book in my collection talks about him. A jovial chap, apparently. He gives every impression of having had a very good evening with plenty of top-class food and, more obviously, wine.

But I could find nobody who had ever seen him. Perhaps the roar of modern traffic has put him off. Or it might be the glare of street lights. Whatever it is that has discouraged him, the ghostly cavalier does not seem to walk the streets of Hook any longer. Unless anyone knows different, of course.

The town of Alton used to be famous for its weaving industry, and was so prosperous that it sent two men to serve as Members of Parliament during the fourteenth century. Weaving is long gone and today Alton is a pretty market town bypassed by the thundering traffic along the A31 dual carriageway. The church is of medieval date, and its twin naves speak volumes for the prosperity of the town in those days, but most of the town buildings date back to Georgian times when the older timber houses were replaced by elegant facades of brick and tile.

One of the buildings constructed at that time that has survived almost unchanged ever since is the Crown Hotel in the town centre. The Crown lies in the High Street, but finding it is not as easy as such an address might indicate – at least, not if you are arriving by car. The one-way system of Alton, and the numerous roads that end in a line of bollards to stop through-traffic, make navigating the town centre rather tricky. It is best to follow signs for the town centre and park the car in the first car park you come to, then walk towards the main shopping streets and ask for the way to the High Street. Once there, the imposing Crown Hotel is easy enough to find.

The ghostly cavalier of Hook seems to be a jovial chap.

On the day I came to Alton, the rain was simply chucking down from low, slate-coloured clouds. Fortunately, the pub is a warm and welcoming place, so much so that when I called the landlord, Peter, went out of his way to show me around.

One of the first places Peter took me to was the cellar bar. It is said to be haunted by a man known only as Patrick. 'We don't know who he is,' said Peter as he led the way down the steep stairs. 'And nobody's seen him either. But we all know he is down there. He moves things about, you know, and messes with the lights and stuff.'

At the bottom of the stairs, I found myself in a spacious, if low, bar. It is used for functions and meetings as a rule. 'I don't like coming down here much,' confided Peter. 'It's okay when

The Crown Hotel in Alton has several ghosts as well as being a most welcoming hostelry.

One of the ghosts at Alton's Crown Hotel haunts this downstairs bar, where the author had an unnerving experience himself.

The haunted fireplace at the Crown Hotel in Alton had a most grisly secret to reveal during recent building works.

there's a few of you, of course, but not on your own.' He switched the lights on and glanced around, then led me to the far wall. 'This is the oldest part of the pub. We think it was built about 1550. Upstairs the old walls are covered up by later decorations, but down here you can see the … Oh.' Peter stopped as the lights were flicked off. There was a moment of silence in the sudden darkness. 'Um', said Peter rather nervously. 'Perhaps we should leave.' Fortunately, there was enough light entering from the lights on the stairs to enable me to find my way back upstairs.

'Right, you'll want to see our haunted bedroom upstairs.' Peter led the way up the main stairs and turned left to the room at the far end of the corridor. 'We haven't got anyone staying in this room today,' he said as he unlocked the door. 'You're lucky.' After my experiences in the cellar, I was not too sure about this, but followed anyway.

'Our lady in here is quite different,' explained Peter. 'She is a serving girl from way back. Very nice, apparently. She just wants to check that everything is neat and tidy, like. She'll pop in to make sure tidying up is done right.'

'Do the guests mind at all?' I asked.

'Oh no. We wouldn't put guests in if there was any bother. She's not seen by guests. Just by the staff. She checks up they've done their job right, you see.'

Peter had left the most famous supernatural event until last. It made all the newspapers a few years ago and even featured on radio. This revolves around the fireplace in the main bar. For many years people in the bar had been hearing strange scratching noises coming from the fireplace. Most put it down to a bird coming down the chimney and being trapped. Little

Alton's Amery Street is haunted by a phantom which might be the shade of perhaps the greatest poet of the sixteenth century.

attention was paid to the noises. Even staff who heard them regularly did not bother much. Just that scratching again, they thought, and got on with their jobs.

Then, in 1967, the pub was going through one of the regular refurbishments that public houses go through. The fireplace was to be converted to one of the electric affairs that were then popular, and this involved channelling the wiring into the wall. As they worked, the men found a cavity behind the wall beside the fireplace. Clearing away the false wall, the men found a small alcove. On the floor lay the skeleton of a dog. How long it had been there, nobody knows. The panelling had been in place as long as anyone could remember.

Leaving the Crown Inn, you need to turn right down the High Street to find the Market Square, then turn right along the eastern side of the square, then right again to enter Amery Street. There is something of a mystery surrounding the ghostly presence in Amery Street. There is no doubt that the ghost is seen; the mystery is whose ghost this might be.

First, the ghost. Some years ago, when I was first looking into the supernatural, I picked up an old, dog-eared book in a second-hand shop in Devon. It was a wide-ranging book detailing ghosts seen across England. The writer of the book was very confident about this particular ghost:

> The spectral visitor to Amery Street in Alton is none other than Edmund Spenser, who lived in this Hampshire town for a good number of years. Dressed in a dark suit and tall hat, he is seen walking down the hill towards the market place. It was at his house in Amery Street that Spenser produced his finest work, revolutionising English poetry by introducing new forms and exhibiting a daring use of archaic language and provincial dialect. There can be no doubt that it is this burgeoning of the poetic muse which brings one of England's finest writers back to his home in Alton some centuries after his untimely death.

The Edmund Spenser referred to was born in London around 1552, the son of a prosperous merchant. He was educated at Merchant Taylor's School and then went up to Cambridge where he earned a name for the poetic manner in which he translated Greek and Roman verse into English. Leaving Cambridge, he got a job in the household of the Earl of Leicester due to influence by his father. Leicester was, at this time, not only astonishingly rich but was a great personal friend of Queen Elizabeth I. Although Spenser's job was a lowly one, it did allow him to hobnob with the great and the good. His party piece, as it were, was to pen a few lines of highly complimentary verse about some visiting nobleman or courtier. Laced with wit and humorous allusions to current affairs and notables, the verses proved to be hugely popular though few survive. On the strength of this work, Spenser was hired as a secretary by Lord Grey de Wilton, who was himself soon made Lord Deputy of Ireland and sent over the Irish Sea to govern that troublesome Kingdom on behalf of Queen Elizabeth. He was rewarded for his work not in cash, but in land, gaining vast estates around Kilcolman and enjoying the rents thereof. Spenser died in 1599, lauded as the greatest-living English poet.

Armed with such confidently stated information, I trotted up Amery Street. The street in question is both short and steep, and on the day I visited it was quiet. Not knowing which of the houses had been Spenser's in his time in Alton, or indeed if the poet's old home was still standing, I did not know where to knock to ask for ghostly information.

Fortunately, the welcoming doors of the Market Hotel were to hand, so I popped in and asked the barman if he knew anything about Edmund Spenser or his ghost. The young man shrugged. 'Dunno', he said. 'I'll ask.'

The barman returned a short time later and indicated a middle-aged man sitting near a window. 'That's Bob, he might know.' I approached Bob and asked about the ghost. 'Well now,' came the reply, 'I don't know anything about a ghost. But Spenser lived up the road true enough. At Number 1, I think it was. He came here when he was in disgrace with Queen Elizabeth.'

This came as news to me. So far as I knew, Spenser was the queen's favourite poet. His work was much more fashionable at court than that of his contemporary, William Shakespeare, who was largely dismissed at this date as a populist playwright penning entertainment for the masses. Indeed, Spenser's most famous work was The Faerie Queen, an enormously long allegory of six books casting Queen Elizabeth in a most flattering light. What could this silver-tongued poet have said wrong?

'He insulted the French Duke de Alenson,' revealed Bob. 'The Queen was being nice to the French at the time and didn't like it when Spenser wrote a poem insulting this important visitor. That's when he came here to lie low for a bit, see.'

This story of a short visit in disgrace did not quite square with the old book that claimed Spenser had written his greatest work here in Alton. I later checked the facts and found that Spenser had written most of The Faerie Queen in his spare time as a young man in Ireland when employed by Lord Grey de Wilton. In 1594, however, he had been in England trying to regain favour at court with a succession of brilliantly written poems, satires and elegies. One of the best was not intended for the court, though it was later published, but was aimed at a Miss Elizabeth Boyle. Dubbed Amoretti, the poem is a skilful declaration of love couched in romantic allusions and allegories. It was followed by the joyful Epithalamion which was first performed at his marriage to Miss Boyle, the courtship having proved successful. It was this work that he apparently penned here in Alton.

Well, that was all some time ago. Rather more current was the story that I had picked up a month or so earlier when I was at a dinner in London. I had got chatting, as one does, to a venerable elderly gent who was sitting to my left. 'Oh yes,' this white-haired army veteran said. 'If you are after ghosts you want to take yourself down to Alton, in Hampshire. If you find Amery Street you

The church at Alton was turned into a fortress in 1643 as a troop of Roundhead cavalry threatened this Royalist town.

might see the ghost of my old granddad dressed in his funeral finest – you know black suit and top hat. That was how we buried him when I was a young lad – just after the Kaiser's War.'

So, Edmund Spenser, internationally known poet and writer, or somebody's old granddad? Whoever the ghost of Amery Street might be, he can be easily spotted by his black suit and tall hat.

There is, however, no doubt about the ghosts to be found at Alton's Church of St Lawrence. To find it, I walked up Amery Street from the Market Square to where it turns sharp right to run down to the High Street. A turning on the left is the aptly named Church Street, and I found the fine church on the left about 200 yards up this street.

Alton has spent most of its centuries-long history slumbering in gentle tranquillity, but on one violent and bloody day in 1643 it leapt to national fame. The fame may have gone, but the marks of the violence remain, both physical and spectral.

During the 1640s, England was torn apart by the Civil War that would see King Charles I sent to the scaffold and end in victory for the Parliamentarian Roundheads of Oliver Cromwell. But in December 1643 the war had only just begun. The King had raised an army from the Midlands and the West Country, while Parliament held London and East Anglia.

The townsfolk of Alton were fiercely Royalist, so they viewed the arrival of a Parliamentarian army in Farnham with unease. Help was at hand, however, for a regiment of infantry and a squadron of cavalry, led by Lord Crawford, rode into town to hold it for the King. Crawford bivouacked his troops in the hop fields that then surrounded the town, and converted the Church of St Lawrence into his command post. At this date the church was the only stone building in what was otherwise a timber town, so it was the natural place to serve as a military strongpoint. It also had the advantage that by camping in the church, the Royalist troopers could be warm and dry without turning any of the loyal townsfolk out of their houses. Firing platforms were built inside each window, allowing musketeers to fire through the glass. Crawford then sent scouts out towards Farnham to keep an eye on the Roundheads.

The battle for control of Alton in 1643 reached a bloody climax in the pulpit of the parish church.

The Parliamentarian commander, however, was the notoriously wily Sir William Waller. He allowed Crawford's scouts to see his men encamped around Farnham and foraging around Bentley. The Roundheads gave every indication of settling down to hold a defensive position. Once he knew that the Royalist scouts had had plenty of time to report back, Crawford marched his main body of men north-west, swinging north of Alton to attack the town down what is now the A339.

Crawford was taken by surprise and hurriedly gave the order to retreat towards Winchester. He left in the town a rearguard of about 100 infantry under Colonel John Boles, with orders to delay Waller's 3,000 men as long as possible before running for it or surrendering.

Boles skirmished through the streets of the town before making his final stand in the church. For several hours his crack musketeers held off the Roundheads, shooting down any that dared to cross the churchyard. Eventually the ammunition ran out and the Roundheads were able to batter down the church doors and burst in.

The enraged Waller gave little quarter and only a few Royalists were taken alive. Colonel Boles was not among them. He took his stand in the pulpit with pistols and sword. It is said he killed six Roundheads before he was cut down. Yet he and his men had not died in vain – the main Royalist force had slipped away from the trap to regroup in Winchester.

The marks of this fight are still seen in the church. The south door has a loophole cut in it from which Royalist musketeers fired at the enemy, and it is pitted by bullet holes. Elsewhere the stonework, especially around the windows, is pockmarked by bullets, some of which remain embedded deep in the stones. When the roof was repaired in the nineteenth century dozens of bullets were retrieved from the old timbers, some of which are on show in a glass case in the church.

I was more interested in the less obvious relics of the grim battle. The ghosts of Boles and his men are said to return to fight their last battle time and again in the churchyard and in the church itself. Several people have reported hearing shouts and cursing as well as the clash of metal on metal and the unmistakable 'phut-bang' of ancient muskets being fired. Some have even reported the smell of burnt gunpowder. The noises of battle begin outside, then move inside and end at the pulpit, still standing, where Colonel Boles died so valiantly.

By the time I got to the church there had been an hour or so of sunshine to dry up the water left by the earlier rain. Nobody much was about, perhaps fearing another heavy shower. I heard no gunfire, nor smelt gunpowder. The Church of St Lawrence stood peaceful and serene within its great churchyard.

This is, perhaps, how it should be. The church dates back to about 1070, having been built in the exciting new Norman style within a few years of the Norman Conquest. This original church remains, though it has been extended to north, west and east over the years. It has not, however, changed much since the day of battle. The west door has been bricked up, but otherwise it stands pretty much as it was when repairs after the battle were completed in 1646. Whether you are hunting ghosts, looking for a historic church or just after somewhere for a quiet moment of peace, the Church of St Lawrence in Alton is well worth a visit.

If the town of Alton has more than its fair share of spooks, it must be said that it is nothing compared to the village of Crondall. Over the years, I have heard more tales in and about this place than any other village in Hampshire. And it is a charming place, too. At least, I have always enjoyed my visits here. The village lies between the A287 and A31, some four miles west from Farnham and is signposted from both these A roads. The High Street is easy to find as the main road through the village runs along it. The church lies to the south of the High Street, beside the large house known as Crondall Lodge. Take the narrow lane beside the Plume of Feathers pub and the church lies on your right, about 200 yards down the lane. Croft Lane runs beside the churchyard, heading east.

Crondall's ghostly soldier runs up this avenue of trees to the church before vanishing abruptly.

The best known of the various phantoms lurking in Crondall is that of a Roundhead trooper who is seen around the church. The sightings of this ghost are fairly consistent with each other and I believe the ghost simply repeats its actions every time it appears.

The first indication of the approaching ghost is the sound of horses' hooves in Croft Lane. Starting faintly as if in the distance, the sound of hooves approaches rapidly from the east. Then a horseman comes into view. He turns his horse through the church gates and rides up to the church doors along the path lined with lime trees. Then he pulls his mount to a halt and leaps to the ground. The man wears body armour of seventeenth-century date over a colourful shirt or jacket, and has great, heavy top boots covering his legs. He hammers at the church door as if demanding immediate admittance, and then he vanishes.

Nobody knows who this ghost in a hurry may be, but he is almost certainly connected to the ghost in the High Street. This man is also in seventeenth-century dress, but this time civilian clothes are on show. Those who see him are sure he is a gentleman. At any rate he wears a sweeping hat with wide brim and a large feather. Opinion is clear that he is a cavalier, in contrast to the presumed Roundhead sympathies of the ghost at the church.

Both phantoms may be something to do with a man who once lived in Crondall High Street, one Nicholas Love. It was this man who paid for the church to be largely rebuilt in the mid-seventeenth century, but this is not why he is linked to the two ghosts.

Mr Love was a staunch Parliamentarian – which put him in the minority in Hampshire – and he was a lawyer. As such, he sat as one of the judges at the trial of King Charles I in 1649. By this date Parliament had won the Civil War and the hard-liners were in power, led by Oliver Cromwell. They had tried to negotiate a deal with Charles, but it was soon revealed that the King was merely playing for time while his wife was abroad trying to hire an army of foreign mercenaries. Determined to be rid of the King and establish a republic, Cromwell and his supporters put the King on trial. He had lost the First Civil War, but then instigated a second conflict, seen as going against God's will. The charges were varied, but boiled down to the fact that he had acted outside the law, had behaved like a tyrant and was unfit to be King.

Love was happy enough to convict the King of all charges; after all, the evidence was fairly convincing, at least for the first two charges. However, like several other judges at the trial, Love had thought that once he had been dethroned the former monarch would either be put in prison or sent into exile. When Cromwell suggested that the King be executed, Love violently disagreed. When Cromwell's troopers arrived at Love's rooms in Whitehall with drawn swords to force his signature on the death warrant, the wily lawyer was nowhere to be found. He was back in Crondall where he very sensibly kept his head down for the next few years.

What business the Cavalier and the Roundhead have with Mr Love is unclear, but it must be important to bring them back to Crondall time after time for over 300 years.

The High Street has another ghost, or rather a whole flock of them. They are without doubt white and woolly ghosts, for they are sheep. When I last called the village was decorated with bunting and flags for a fête, but nobody knew of the ghostly sheep.

'You want to get up to the church,' said one old chap that I stopped to talk to. 'They do say there is a ghostly horseman up there. But I don't hear of any ghostly sheep.' Perhaps the cavalier has driven them all away.

Murder was done at Kingsclere, but it was hushed up so effectively that the story took years to come out. But the ghost knows and will make clear what happened for those brave enough to ask. The modern A339 now bypasses the village centre, so if approaching by car it is necessary to turn off down the B3051 towards Overton. Once in Kingsclere, the pub is easy to find as it occupies a prominent position beside the surgery, opposite the church and within sight of the village shops.

I came to Kingsclere on a chilly, windy day as scudding clouds threatened to bring rain to

The High Street of Crondall has a number of ghosts, of which the most unusual is the phantom sheep.

the Hampshire countryside. I had a lot of ground to cover, for other ghost stories beckoned, so I arrived at the Crown at Kingsclere soon after noon. I asked the landlord about the haunting, which he knew all about.

The trouble began in the early months of 1944. The house and grounds of nearby Sydmonton Court had been commandeered for the war effort and transformed into a gigantic camp for US servicemen. Far from home, bored and in imminent danger of sudden death, the soldiers indulged in boisterous fun and some alarmingly high-spirited activities. For the good folk of Kingsclere that was bad enough, but when an outbreak of burglaries and shoplifting took place it was too much. The village policeman passed on the concerns to his superiors and a squad of American Military Police began frequent patrols. A local girl was then raped after befriending one of the soldiers.

The villagers decided to ban the US soldiers from the shops and pubs of the village centre and generally to cold shoulder them. Of course, the units stationed at the camp came and went with great frequency as the countdown to D-Day began, so entirely innocent newcomers were blamed and punished for the acts of men who had moved on to other places.

Unfortunately, one unit that came to Sydmonton was composed of black soldiers, or Negro GIs as they were then termed. These men mistook the behaviour of the villagers for the sort of outright racism they had experienced in the US Deep South. They resented it. One day a group of ten black soliders got hold of some whisky, and after drinking a good deal of it they wandered into Kingsclere.

Arriving at the Crown, the drunken men entered demanding to be served. The landlady, Mrs Rosa Napper, refused and called on three Military Policemen to oust the soldiers. The MPs asked for the men's papers and, when a couple could not produce them, ordered the whole group back to the camp.

By now the ten men were angry, resentful and drunk. They grabbed their rifles and opened fire on the pub from the churchyard opposite. First to fall was Mrs Napper, shot through the

A horrific double murder took place at the Crown at Kingsclere in 1944, but it was hushed up for political reasons. The ghost, however, has always refused to be silenced.

The church at Kingsclere, seen from the front door of the Crown. The fatal shots came from behind the wall just to the left of the pollarded tree.

The ghostly Mrs Rosa Napper is seen most often in this corridor leading to the function room of the Crown at Kingsclere.

neck as she leant against the front bar. An MP was shot through the head and died instantly, while a second was mortally wounded. The third MP returned fire, bringing down two GIs and persuading the rest to flee. The village policeman and a sergeant from Overton joined the chase and within hours all the soldiers had been arrested. Mrs Napper died later in hospital.

The soldiers were court-martialled and sentenced to life imprisonment back in the USA. The case caused a sensation. Kingsclere was not the only place where tensions existed between locals and the US servicemen. The fact that the men involved were all black seriously alarmed the government, as ethnic minorities were then rare in England and nobody knew how people might react. The Government decided that the whole matter had to be hushed up as quickly as possible. Even the local newspapers were persuaded not to print details, and the national papers did not mention the incident at all.

But the phantom of Mrs Napper knew all about the killing, and she was not going to rest. Within a few weeks of her death, the ghost of Mrs Napper began to be seen at the pub. No shrinking violet this, the ghost walked boldly about the Crown, as solid as could be. She was seen in the bar and in the restaurant. But the ghost was seen most often walking along the corridor behind the bar that leads to the restaurant and the private quarters. Here the ghost strides along, forcing those she encounters to step out of her way. Even sixty years on, Mrs Napper is a powerful figure.

By now the pub was beginning to fill up with the lunchtime trade. I slipped off to inspect the haunted corridor and the restaurant. 'We still see her quite a lot,' the landlord said. 'She walks down the corridor towards the bar, you see. I suppose somebody sees her every two or three months or so.'

WINCHESTER AND THE SURROUNDING AREA

Almost certainly an important centre for the local Belgae tribe of Celts by around 200 BC, Winchester first enters written history as a major administrative centre in Roman times. The city was then known as Venta Belgarum, and was laid out in typically Roman fashion with a grid of streets arranged around two main thoroughfares that formed a T-shape. This plan is still clear to this day. The city was surrounded by stout walls in the third century when barbarian raids became more common, and they were to serve the city well in the centuries that followed.

Winchester is unique among the major Roman cities of Britain in that it never fell to the English invaders who swamped the island in the years after 449. Canterbury was handed over by treaty, and so did not fall in war, but it still passed to the English invaders. Winchester, however, took a different course. The area was ruled by a council of local rich men, as was usual in Roman Britain, and by the 490s one family and one man had come to dominate. We are not certain quite what position Cerdic held, but he seems to have been the chief magistrate of the city and surrounding area. In 490, or 510 according to some sources, Cerdic announced that Venta Belgarum would no longer recognise the authority of the self-appointed governors who were running Britain after the Roman Emperors had pulled out eighty years or so before. Cerdic hired a powerful force of English mercenaries to ensure that the governors could not re-impose their rule by force.

In the decades that followed, Cerdic's successors continued his pro-English policy, inviting in more soldiers and settlers. By 650 they had become English-style Kings, speaking English in a land mostly inhabited by English-speakers, though recent genetic research indicates that the area was still some 80 per cent British. They had forgotten their Christian religion and adopted the pagan gods of the English, but were soon to convert back again when that became politically convenient.

The land became known as Wessex, the land of the Western Saxons, and as such is generally known today. Winchester takes its name from the Roman phrase 'Venta Castrum', meaning the fortified place at Venta. As the Kings of Wessex expanded their realm to include all of England, Winchester became the royal capital. Coronations took place here, and the royal treasury was located in the city. London was always larger and more wealthy, but administration was carried out from Winchester.

By the time of the Norman Invasion, Winchester was as English a city as you could hope to find. Its subsequent history has been similar to that of many another English cities. Its importance in royal administration gradually waned as Kings preferred to be based closer to the financial centre of London, but its magnificent cathedral was lavishly endowed by a succession of monarchs who recognised the important of the city.

Winchester Cathedral is surely the most popular building in the city. It is among the largest and the oldest of Winchester's many tourist attractions, it has been celebrated in music and has featured on postcards sent to almost every country on earth.

Winchester Cathedral is surely the most popular building in the city, and one of the most haunted.

So popular is it that visitors come back time and again to wonder at its beauty and majestic setting. Some come back more often than others. One has been coming back at intervals for the past 600 years. He simply cannot get enough of the cathedral.

The phantom in question, for a ghost he undoubtedly is, is that of a monk. He seems to feel the attractions of the cathedral more strongly at some times than at others. He was seen frequently in the post-war years and again in the 1970s, but at other times rarely puts in an appearance more than once a year.

If the frequency of his appearances are irregular, his habits — if you will pardon the pun — are not. He slowly materialises out of nothingness in the southern end of the close, near to house No.11. Having become solid, the phantom moves across the close towards the arch which forms a roadway to the gardens near the South Transept.

Yet this ghost does not glide in the approved fashion of ghosts. He limps. And he limps quite badly. No footsteps are heard, but those who have seen the ghostly monk notice that he almost drags his right foot as he moves across the close. Continuing his painful progress, the monk approaches the arch and then fades from sight. Some claim he passes through the arch, others that he shimmers and slips away into a misty form that vanishes to nothing.

I came to the cathedral on a bright spring day when there was still a hint of winter in the chill breeze. Office workers and shop staff were munching on sandwiches in the cathedral close and on the green in front of the great West Front. There were some tourists too, but they were intent on getting into the cathedral, or out again and on to the next tourist site.

Most of the sandwich scoffers knew little or nothing of the ghostly monk. Though one young woman ventured, 'Oh, yeah. Some chap took a photo of the ghost in the cathedral. I've seen it in a book.' This, in fact, was a quite different ghost entirely, of a medieval workman, but that is another story.

The Cathedral Close at Winchester is haunted by a limping monk. The phantom usually first appears close to the house to the right of this picture, then limps across the lawn to vanish beside an arch just out of shot to the left.

Finally, I found someone who knew of the spectral cathedral monk. 'My brother saw it once,' declared a middle-aged gentleman in a well-cut tweed jacket. 'Nothing very frightening about it though. Just a monk walking to the cathedral. He didn't even have his head under his arm.' But then very few ghosts do appear as the popular stories would have us imagine. When was this? 'Oh some years ago now. The 1970s? Could be, could be.'

Quite how old the phantom might be is rather unclear. Winchester Cathedral is one of the oldest religious foundations in England. As the centre of the old Kingdom of Wessex, Winchester was the home of the Kingdom's most prestigious religious building since the conversion of Wessex in the seventh century. The foundations of the early English cathedral can be seen traced out on the green besides the present building.

The mighty cathedral we see today was largely the work of the Normans, who tore down the old church and erected their own in majestic stone to mark the start of the new regime. The church was extended in the thirteenth century and in the fourteenth was remodelled in the then fashionable Perpendicular Gothic. Throughout all this time, the cathedral was served by monks. Only after Henry VIII's Dissolution in the sixteenth century did the monks leave the cathedral to the clergy. In theory the phantom monk might date back to any century from the seventh to the sixteenth.

But there is one clue. During one of the periods of alterations that take place around the cathedral from time to time, a number of burials were unearthed in what is now a private garden, but was evidently once part of the cathedral precincts. The bodies were all male and date to about the fourteenth century. They were probably monks.

What does this have to do with our phantom? Well, one of the bodies had a grossly deformed arthritic right knee. It would have given him a very bad limp.

There are plenty of stories about the old cathedral and its monks. The holy brethren were famously inventive. Cathedrals and priories cost a lot of money to maintain and beautify, and as any good Christian could tell you, 'the poor are always with us.' So the monks did, perhaps, have a need to be rather more inventive than most when it came to raising funds.

That, at least, is what Bishop Walkelyn thought back in 1079. He was rather fed up with the slightly dilapidated state of the old cathedral. When compared to some of the newer cathedrals being erected across northern Europe in the Norman style, Winchester Cathedral was decidedly small and unimpressive. And Winchester was the most important city in England at the time. So Bishop Walkelyn got permission from King William I to go to the New Forest and cut down some wood to use in building a new cathedral. 'Take as much as you and your men can cut in four days,' said the King.

When he got back to Winchester, Bishop Walkelyn took a look at his collection of monks. In four days, they would probably be able to cut down enough wood to build a shed, which was, of course, what King William had thought when making his promise. But the bishop was a clever man. He went out and rounded up every able-bodied man in Hampshire he could lay hands on. He inducted them as lay brothers, then sent them out for the stipulated four days. They cut down so many trees that great swathes of the New Forest close to Winchester simply ceased to exist.

King William was not impressed, but Winchester got its new cathedral.

Nor was the cathedral the only thing the wily monks got their hands on. The thing about monks, back in the twelfth century, was that they could read and write when few other people could do so. And all deeds to land were written down. When somebody died without leaving heirs, it was surprising how often the monks managed to find a deed or will stating that the land of the deceased had been left to them!

Which brings us to the ghosts of St George Street. According to an old book I chanced across in the library, the patch of land on the corner of that street, and what is now Royal Oak Passage, was one such patch of land which was acquired by the monks. They consecrated the land and set it aside for the burial of their holy brothers, building a small chapel on the site.

Before long the sight of a procession of monks carrying the body of one of their own became familiar to the people of Winchester. The group came out of the cathedral precincts, crossed High Street and turned up St George's Street to reach the burial plot. The sombre duty done, the monks processed back down High Street.

Then came the Reformation in the sixteenth century, as ordered by King Henry VIII. Not even the wily monks of Winchester could escape that particular event. The cathedral chapter and the priory were closed down to be replaced by Church of England organisations. The funeral processions of the monks came to an end.

Or rather, they did not. There are scattered accounts of the funeral processions being recreated in spectral form in several old histories of Winchester. One, from about 1640, talks of the procession marching sombrely with chanting monks, clanging hand bells and flapping sacred banners. Later accounts are less dramatic. A Victorian writes of shadowy figures lurking around what was once the burial ground. These days, there seems to be just one lone monk left of this grand procession.

Having got as far as I could in the library, I went to the old burial plot to see what could be found on a bright sunny day. The first few passers-by knew nothing of the ghosts. Then one chap came along who seemed to know all about it.

'Oh yes,' he said. 'The phantom monk. You're in the wrong place.' He led me round the corner into Royal Oak Passage. 'This is where he's seen. Walks slowly from one end to the other, then vanishes.' Had the man seen the ghost himself? 'Well, no. But my mate Stuart did.' I handed over a card and asked if Stuart would call me.

Nobody else out and about in Winchester that afternoon seemed to know much about the ghost, though one lady had heard of him. My mobile phone then rang. It was Stuart:

Winchester's Royal Oak Passage is a narrow alley between buildings fronting the High Street. It is also the haunt of a most alarming phantom.

The ghostly monk of Royal Oak Passage, based on an eyewitness description given to the author.

That's right, the monk ghost chap. It was one evening last summer. I'd finished work and was walking back to my car when I cut down that alley by the pub. Nobody else around at the time. The shoppers had all gone home and the night life hadn't got going. Then I saw this figure coming towards me dressed in a long cloak and hood. I thought it was a bit odd 'cos it was a warm evening. Nobody would need to wrap up like that. Then, when we were passing each other, I felt suddenly cold. Like if you stand under the air conditioning unit in a shop. There was this cold draft. I looked round to see what could have caused it, then realised the figure had gone. There was nowhere he could have gone, you see. He was only a couple of feet away from me. Then he was gone.

It was not a warm evening by this time, so I buttoned up my coat before heading onto Royal Oak Passage again. The sun was dipping down and dusk was gathering. I looked about. No phantom monk was in sight, but it was a very atmospheric place. Just the sort of place you would expect to meet something odd.

I nearly jumped out of my skin when I got a tap on the shoulder. It was no phantom monk, however, but the barman from the Royal Oak.

'I heard you talking about ghosts,' he said. 'The pub is haunted, you know. And there was some right weird stuff going on here this morning. Come back in and talk to Gina, the manageress. I'll get her for you.'

The barman led me back into the bar and took me to a lady cleaning glasses. 'This bloke is interested in ghosts,' said the barman. 'I thought you could tell him about our phantom. I mean, it's been a bit odd from time to time, but this morning was real bad.'

Gina looked surprised, 'You didn't say.'

'Yeah, well,' replied her barman. 'Happens so often there's no point mentioning it any longer.'

I was interested and asked for details. Apparently it is not at all unusual for the electrical equipment located in the upstairs office to be interfered with when nobody is about. The multi-track CD system which ensures the bar receives a constantly changing selection of soothing background music is sometimes switched off when it should be on, or switched on when it should be off. Or the play list is altered. Perhaps the phantom here is a keen music fan.

Then there is the computer which logs stock control, wages and other matters. That often goes on and off of its own accord. Then there are the lights in the office. Sometimes they are on, sometimes off, but nobody ever seems to be about when they are switched. Strangely, the lights do not seem to be on when the music system is changed. Presumably our spectre does not need to see what he or she is doing.

But who is this mischievous spirit? Gina, the manageress, had been looking for some answers before I turned up. She had been down the local library poring over the old property records

The Royal Oak in Winchester is plagued by a most troublesome phantom, who gets up to his tricks most often in the older, two-storey part of the building.

for Winchester to see what she could turn up. She found that the older part of the building, near the High Street, had been owned by the cathedral priory since some time in the mid-eleventh century. Indeed, there is an old stone arch in the lower bar which probably dates from about this time. It is protected by planning law, in any case.

The cathedral monks kept the building for their own use for some generations. There was a tunnel which ran from the cellar to the priory cellar. Gina thinks the monks brewed beer in her cellar, then trundled the barrels down the tunnel to their own stores. Very sneaky. And it might explain why the monks called the place 'Beau Repaire', meaning it was a nice place to visit. In any case, in 1323 the building was rented to a chap called Peter of Exeter and he most certainly did use the cellar for brewing beer. This gives the building a good claim to be the oldest bar in England, certainly in Winchester. That said, the main building above ground level seems to date from about 1630.

Rather more interesting from the point of view of identifying the music-loving spectre is the fact that the end of the building facing St George's Street is much newer, being only about 350 years old. Before the Reformation, in the sixteenth century, the land on which it stands had been part of the burial ground for the cathedral monks. Could this explain our phantom? Certainly the monks were well known for their love of music and singing.

We shall probably have to wait to see if anyone ever sees the ghost at his work to find out who he really is. Meanwhile, if you visit the Royal Oak and find the music suddenly stops or repeats the same song endlessly, don't blame the staff. It's just the ghost up to his old tricks.

At the other end of town from the cathedral is the Theatre Royal on Jewry Street, which has almost as many ghosts to its name as the cathedral with its various phantom monks. In 2004 the local press was filled with stories of a rash of sightings of phantoms in the building, so I decided to pay a visit.

'The ghost? Oh yes. Which one?' smiled the receptionist at Winchester's Theatre Royal when I told her of the reason for my dropping in.

'Err. How many have you got?' I asked. I had read of one ghost at the theatre, but now it seemed as if there might be more than one.

'Three,' came the reply. 'Well, four if you like. But we don't count the old lady. She's a left over from before the theatre was built.'

I was most intrigued. I awaited the arrival of Phil Yates. Mr Yates, the receptionist had said, knew all about the ghosts. He did. It seems that the most active ghost at the Theatre Royal is the 'Man in Black', who haunts the circle. He is usually seen after the evening's show is over and most of the public have gone home. He appears quite solid and normal. More than one usher, clearing up after the public, has mistaken him for a loitering theatre-goer. Until he walks through a wall, that is.

The Man in Black is the ghost of John Simpkins, brother of James Simpkins who opened the theatre back in 1914. It seems that James was the artistic one who put on the shows and hobnobbed with the greats of the early twentieth-century stage. John was the brother with business sense. He left running the theatre to James, but would visit regularly after the show to go through the books and count the money. He had a small, private office located just off the circle where he would do his work. The room is now used for storage and the door that led on to the circle has long since been blocked up. John died in the early 1920s, but James continued to run the theatre until the mid-1930s.

When John lay dying he asked his brother one last favour. Over the stage at the Theatre Royal was a cartouche with the initials 'J S'. These could be taken to mean John Simpkins or James Simpkins, but now John wanted the letters altered to read 'J & J S', to make it clear that there had been two brothers. James agreed, but after John died he either forgot his promise or

Winchester's Theatre Royal stands on Jewry Street and is home to an interesting collection of phantoms.

found the work would have been too pricey. The lettering was never changed. Perhaps it is this broken promise which brings the ghostly John Simpkins back to the theatre.

The spectral John Simpkins lurks about the circle and his old office. He does not know the doorway between the two has gone, which is why he still walks through it, appearing and disappearing through the solid wall. He also likes to walk along the rear of the circle from the entrance stairs to what was his office. So often is the figure in black seen here, that the route is known to staff as 'the Ghost Walk'.

The second ghost has a more tragic story. Young Jim worked in the theatre as a lime boy, meaning that he operated the lime lights that served as modern spotlights do today. In 1915 this young chap joined up to serve in the Great War and marched off to the trenches in France. He left behind him not only his widowed mother, but also his sweetheart Lucy who worked as one of the chorus girls at the theatre.

One night in 1916 the music hall show was playing to a full house. The chorus line came on, then suddenly collapsed into confusion when Lucy stopped still instead of dancing. The girl turned as white as a sheet, then ran off the stage. The manager found her sobbing uncontrollably off-stage.

'I've seen Jim,' the girl gasped. 'He was standing by the limelight, just like he always used to.'

'But you can't have,' said James Simpkins. 'He's in France and not due home on leave for weeks yet.'

'I know,' sobbed Lucy. 'Then he waved goodbye to me and just faded away.'

A few days later, Jim's mother received a telegram from the War Office telling her that her son had been killed in the trenches. He had been shot at almost the precise moment he had appeared at the Theatre Royal.

Which brings us to the third ghost. A vague female wraith has been seen on the stage from time to time. Is it Lucy the chorus girl? We do not know. The ghost always appears only vaguely and soon drifts off to nothingness.

The Ghost Walk area of the circle at
the Theatre Royal in Winchester is the
favoured haunt of The Man in Black,
said to be the ghost of John Simpkins
who founded the theatre back in 1914.

A play in rehearsal on the stage of
Winchester's Theatre Royal. In 1916 a
chorus girl named Lucy was on stage
when she saws a ghost in the wings.

As for the old lady, she was sensed by the entertainer Michael Benteen when he performed at the Theatre Royal a few years ago. She was dressed in very old-fashioned clothes and seemed to be from a house nearby, and thought she was walking in the garden when, in fact, she was in the stalls bar. The theatre was built in the gardens of Tower House, a fine pile which was erected in the 1700s and survived until about 1985. Perhaps she is the ghost of some long-dead inhabitant of the Tower House who still wanders through what, for her, are lovely gardens.

In popular imagination, ghost stories are tales of dark deeds and terrible deaths. In my experience, this is far from the truth. Most ghosts are of perfectly ordinary people doing perfectly normal things and cause very little bother to the living. But the ghost at The Eclipse public house lives up to the gruesome imagination to the very fullest. The story is a tale of violence, treachery and ghastly revenge. The Eclipse lies in a street known as The Square. This narrow thoroughfare runs from Great Minster Street to the High Street. The projecting pub sign makes this black and white half-timbered building one of the most prominent in the street.

The tale begins back in the 1630s, when a Cornishman named John Penrudduck was hauled up in front of the Winchester courts on charges of theft and seditious conduct. The details of the charges have been lost, but Penrudduck seems to have been agitating against the autocratic rule of King Charles I and to have helped himself to some royal goods by way of protest. The presiding judge was one Sir John Lisle of Moyles Court. When the man was found guilty, Lisle handed down the sentence of death which the laws of the day prescribed.

Ten years later the Lisles were prospering. Sir John was a staunch friend and colleague of Oliver Cromwell, the great Parliamentarian general who swept to victory in the English Civil Wars. Egged on by his wife, Lady Alicia, Sir John sat as one of the judges at the trial of King Charles I for treason. With Cromwell's armed troopers deciding who was to give evidence, and fingering their sword blades, there was only one verdict possible. Once again Sir John sent a man to his death for treason. Lady Alicia attended the execution and wrote that 'my blood leaped within me to see the tyrant fall.'

But already the wheels of fate were turning and vengeance was coming to find the Lisles.

In 1660 the executed King's son came to the throne as King Charles II. Sir John Lisle very wisely fled abroad to escape whatever punishment the new King had in mind. He did not flee far enough. One day Sir John was recognised in a Swiss street by a visiting Englishman, who promptly whipped out a dagger and stabbed Sir John through the heart.

Dame Alicia had stayed in England to look after the family estates and business ventures. Hearing the news of her husband's death, she appeared to retire to her home at Moyles Court. In reality she kept anopen house for the radical Protestants who opposed the new King. In 1685 Charles died and was replaced by his unpopular brother James II. For radicals such as Dame Alicia, this was an opportunity to revive the extreme Protestant views of her beloved Cromwell. She welcomed to her home the preacher John Hickes and the radical lawyer Richard Nelthorp.

The two men were on the run after taking part in the failed rebellion of the Duke of Monmouth. Hot on their tracks came one of King James's most trusted cavalry commanders, a man named Colonel John Penrudduck, son of the man hanged so many years earlier by Sir John Lisle. The presence of the two fugitives was betrayed to Penrudduck by a local Royalist. The colonel led his men to Moyles Court and arrested the two men and Dame Alicia.

Hauled up in front of the notoriously bloodthirsty Judge Jeffries, Dame Alicia could have expected little mercy. In vain did she protest that she had had no idea the two men had been involved in the Monmouth rebellion. Jeffries ordered the jury to find her guilty, which they promptly did. Jeffries sentenced her to be dragged through Winchester on a wooden hurdle, then burnt at the stake in the square.

The Eclipse Inn in Winchester. The scaffold for Lady Lisle's execution was erected directly in front of the building.

The ghost of Lady Lisle is seen most often in this upstairs corridor of the Eclipse Inn, Winchester.

The barbarity of the sentence was too much for the people of Winchester. They organised an appeal to King James. Messengers were sent to London and Dame Alicia was lodged in the upstairs rooms of the Eclipse Inn, with the watchful Colonel Penrudduck and his men keeping armed guard. When the answer came, it stated that the King had decided to be merciful. Dame Alicia would not be burnt – she would be beheaded instead. A scaffold was built outside the Eclipse and one morning Dame Alicia stepped out of her first-floor window on to the wooden platform where she was executed.

When I called at the Eclipse they had just opened for lunch. A couple of early clients were sat at a table, but the main rush of office and shop workers had yet to arrive. The bar staff happily showed me up the staircase to the first floor, where the ghost of Lady Alice, as they called her, is so often seen.

'You don't see much, as a rule,' said the barman, 'even when she is about. There is a grey shape like a lady in a cloak that moves about the upstairs rooms. She never says anything, just drifts around.'

It did not sound the most spectacular of hauntings, but a cleaner who used to work at the pub had another story:

I saw her twice. The first time was when I walked upstairs to do some cleaning. I turned the corner into the passage and there she was staring at me. It gave me a right turn. She had these really bright eyes and was just staring, staring, staring. I found something else to do for a bit and when I came back upstairs she was gone. Second time I saw her, she was in one of the bedrooms. She was dressed in a long grey dress with long, wide sleeves. She just seemed to be looking out the window. She was only there for a second or two, then she vanished. Poof, just gone.

An old book in Winchester Library records several other sightings. One tells how a man was staying in the pub some years ago. In the middle of the night he was woken up by a tall, sinister woman standing at the end of his bed. When she vanished into thin air, the man bolted downstairs and spent the rest of the night sitting awake in the bar. A naval officer had a similar experience, but he fled not just the room but the entire building.

If you are at the theatre's end of town, you could do worse than seek out the Hyde Tavern. From the theatre, head north to cross the main road of North Walls and enter Hyde Street. The Hyde Tavern is on the right about 150 yards past the road junction.

Many years ago, when the Hyde Tavern stood just outside the north gate in the city walls of Winchester, an old woman came calling. It was a chilly winter's evening and the bright sky promised a sharp frost. Pulling her ragged cloak about her, the woman entered the warm, cosy interior of the pub. She ordered a snack and paid for it with her last pennies. As the evening drew to an end, the publican began to lock up after his customers. The old woman begged to be allowed to sleep in the bar, for she had no money to pay for a night's accommodation in one of the bedrooms. The landlord of the day – clearly a hard-hearted sort of a chap – refused and threw the woman out into the street.

The next morning the woman's body was found frozen solid outside the Hyde Tavern. She had died of cold and hunger in the bitter freezing cold of the winter's night.

It was not long before strange things started to happen at the Hyde Tavern. Guests staying in the bedrooms would wake up in the middle of the night feeling extremely cold. Their bed clothes were lying on the floor, allowing the cold air to reach their bodies. A few people mentioned it to the landlord, but thought they had merely kicked the bedclothes off themselves.

Then came the night when a man was lying awake at night, his mind turning over some problem that he had to solve. To his amazement he felt his bedclothes suddenly tugged off him and hurled to the floor. Hurriedly striking a light to see by, the man found himself utterly alone, but the blankets were still twitching.

The bedclothes-snatching has continued ever since. One former landlord in the 1960s had great trouble with the phantom who removed his bedclothes with annoying regularity. Even when he tucked the blankets in securely, they would sometimes end up on the floor.

Then there are the odd goings-on in the front bar. I was perched on a stool in the bar chatting to the barman when the subject came up. I had heard of the blanket-stealing phantom, but not of any spectre in the public parts of the tavern. He mentioned:

Oh yes. It happens quite a lot, usually in the evening. We'll be serving here when somebody will call to be served. But nobody needs serving. It even happens when the pub is empty. I'll sit round the back watching the TV. Then there'll be the sound of someone moving about in the Front Bar here and I'd swear they call. But when I come through. Nobody here. And that's not all. Sometimes people sitting at the bar here will feel somebody tap them on the shoulder. Weird, eh?

But it is not just the Hyde Tavern that is haunted. The street outside has its ghost, perhaps of the old woman who haunts the pub. A Mr Tompkins contacted me back in 2002 to tell of his eerie experience:

About five or six years ago, when I was renting a house in Hyde Street I used to walk to work in the square along Jewry Street. One morning I was walking to work at about 5am in the morning.

Winchester's Hyde Tavern was the scene for a tragic death three or four centuries ago that still has phantasmal repercussions to this day.

The front bar at the Hyde Tavern is the centre for the spooky goings on in this ancient pub.

The haunted stretch of the Andover Road leading out of Winchester. The fatal gibbet stood close to this road junction, though its exact location has been forgotten.

> An old lady approached me from the doorway. Dressed in cloak and hood. She had very sharp facial features. As I approached her she was mumbling to herself and walked straight past me. At this point I turned round, she then fell into the road as if intending to cross. At the same time as a lorry was coming from the High Street. As I turned again it ran straight over the old woman. But she had completely vanished. This terrified me at the time.

For the next ghost of Winchester you will need to find the Andover Road leading out of Winchester. Fortunately, this is fairly straightforward as it is, after all, the road leading from Winchester to Andover. Once out of the one-way system, you are on the correct road. If you are relying on a map, however, look for the B3420, for that is the road you need. The haunted section of the road runs from the crest of North Hill down to the city centre. The Jolly Farmer pub is the most visible landmark along the road.

Now, the word 'rogue' might have been invented for Henry Robert Whitley. Unfortunately for Whitley, the word 'loveable' was not anywhere near as appropriate. This fact was to lead to his death, and to the haunting of an otherwise utterly blameless stretch of road near Winchester.

Whitley lived in Winchester in the early seventeenth century, a period of history when the certainties of the Tudors was giving way to the upheavals of the Stuarts. Civil War was not far away. Political matters did not bother Henry Whitley. He was much more concerned with his neighbours' property, and how he could get his hands on it.

Any citizen of Winchester who left his front door unlocked might find that something had gone missing by the time he got home. Anyone foolish enough to carry money in his purse was likely to find it gone by the time he got to the shops. And there was rarely much doubt as to where it had gone. Whitley was usually around somewhere. Not that anyone wanted him around. He was not only light-fingered, but unpleasant with it. There was no charm to redeem him as a companion, no ready wit and no good looks. He was, to put it bluntly, a bad man.

The Jolly Farmer pub on the Andover Road is the haunt of the ghost of a rather unpleasant rogue by the name of Henry Robert Whitley.

But Whitley was not stupid and he rarely, if ever, got caught. The sense of frustration among the good folk of Winchester during the 1630s can be imagined.

Then, in 1637, Whitley made his fatal mistake. He got caught with stolen goods in his little cottage. Not only had he been seen near the scene of the crime, he had the pilfered goods in his possession. He was quickly hauled up in front of the Quarter Sessions and swiftly found guilty by his fellow citizens. The judge, knowing the man before him, reached for the black cap that signalled death.

In desperation, Whitley pleaded 'Benefit of Clergy'. Although removed from the law books by 1637, the custom that clergymen should not be executed no matter what their crime was still followed. Imprisonment, flogging and branding was their punishment. The judge was, to say the least, surprised. He had no idea that Whitley had ever been ordained, nor did he want to waste time trying to find out. Instead, the judge picked up an edition of the Gospels and threw it across the court room to Whitley.

'Read it', commanded the judge.

Whitley could not read, and stood there silent. The judge donned his black cap and pronounced the awful sentence of death. The next day, Whitley was led from Winchester Gaol to his place of execution. He was hanged from the gibbet on top of North Hill on the Andover Road. When dead, his body was taken down to be wrapped in chains and rehoisted. His rotting corpse swung in the wind for many days to warn all those approaching Winchester what the citizens would do to habitual criminals. Eventually the bones were taken down and thrown into a pauper's grave.

Which was when the hauntings began.

The lone figure of Henry Robert Whitley was seen walking from the gaol out of the city and up to the gibbet on North Hill. Long after the gibbet was taken down, the phantom of Whitley continued to retrace his last mortal journey on this earth. And he walks still.

I retraced those same steps myself when I visited on a windy but sunny afternoon. I found the Andover Road and set off to walk up to North Hill. Finally I reached the hill crest, near the

The lanes around Braishfield are haunted by a miserly old lady who is searching for her lost hoard of gold.

junction with Bereweeke Road, where the gibbet once stood. There was nothing there to mark the spot. There was, however, a pub – the Jolly Farmer. Someone there might know about the ghost, I reasoned. In any case, the uphill walk had been a brisk one and refreshment beckoned.

Pat, the landlady, knew all about the ghost. 'That's right,' she confirmed, 'Old Whitley walks up the road there. Some say that he comes in here, but I can't say as I've ever seen him.' It was busy in the Jolly Farmer, so I did not bother Pat further. There was a notice hanging on the bar wall giving details of the case, so I read it as I sipped my cider. Clearly someone had taken the trouble to find out the details about Whitley, even making a copy of the court records from the Quarter Sessions of 1637. I was surprised to find out that the final crime for which Whitley had been sent to his death was the theft of twelve turkeys, three hens, seven capons and a sack.

Even further out of the city, you might come across the phantom of another notoriously acquisitive local. Braishfield lies west of Winchester. Take the A3090 from Winchester towards Romsey. Leave this road at Standon and follow the lanes to Braishfield, if you know the way. It is less confusing to take the long way round. Stay on the A3090 until you are almost in Romsey, when a road to the right is signposted 'Braishfield'. Follow this road for about two miles and you pass the sign advising you that you are entering the village – a spread-out straggling sort of a place.

There is a ghost here, and this ghost brings with her the promise of great riches – but only if you are brave enough. A century ago, when King Edward VII sat on the throne, a very rich old woman lived in Braishfield. The scale of her wealth was legendary, as was her meanness. The locals called her 'the Miser of Braishfield', and they wondered why on earth she did not spend more of her money.

The old woman shuffled about the village in worn and patched old clothes. Her dresses were so old-fashioned that they dated back to when Queen Victoria had been young. She never took out her carriage, although she had one, if she could walk instead. Shoe leather was cheap enough, but if she took out the carriage she might have to pay her odd-job man extra for the work.

The haunted table in the Wheatsheaf at Braishfield has been the focus for a number of odd events.

That was another thing. She had no live-in servants, though most people of a fraction her wealth did so. Instead, she hired a local woman to come in twice a week to deal with housework. For any heavy work she had a man from the village who would come in when required. From time to time both these staff would tell tales about the old woman and her money. Sometimes she would sneak into the house carrying a leather bag or small box which had earth and mud stuck to it. Clearly it had just been dug up. The old woman would retire into her parlour and then would come the steady chink-chunk of heavy gold coins being counted out.

Back in the early twentieth century gold sovereigns were still in circulation and it was not at all unusual for people to have gold on hand. But nobody has as much gold as the Miser of Braishfield. And it was all divided up in small bags and boxes and buried.

The day came when the old miser died. A nephew came from some miles away to sell the house and contents and to arrange the funeral. But no matter how hard he searched the house nor how thoroughly he dug up the garden, he never found any gold. So he buried his miserly aunt and left.

And that was when the ghost began to walk.

On bright afternoons, dull evenings and even late at night the shuffling figure of the Miser of Braishfield was seen moving around the lanes of the village. Sometimes she was seen poking about in hedges, or thrusting her stick into hollow trees. Thinking the ghost was looking for her lost gold, the villagers tried digging where she was seen. But no gold has been found. At least, none that anyone will talk about.

It was a brilliant spring day when I came to Braishfield to look for the miser. The sun shone bright, though there was still a chilly nip in the wind that blew down the lanes where the ghostly miser wanders. One passer-by knew of the phantom.

'Oh her,' he chuckled when I stopped him. 'Yeah, she's around somewhere. Not that I've ever found any gold. But good luck. If you find the treasure you can buy me a drink. I'll be in the pub having lunch.'

I spent a happy half hour strolling the lanes around Braishfield. It really is a very pretty place and there is a comfortable bench beside the pond where you can rest, and a quaint church to look around if you prefer.

By then I felt it was time for lunch, and made my way to the Wheatsheaf near the centre of the straggling village. The landlord, Peter Jones, was most welcoming. And he had news for me.

'You don't want to waste your time walking around the village,' he said. 'We've got our own ghost here.' He pointed at a table in the corner of the front bar. 'Early in the morning we sometimes see a shape lurking over there. Not sure what it is. Just a shape. And sometimes the table and chairs have been moved overnight as if phantom revellers have been sitting there eating or drinking.'

THE NEW FOREST

A small but charming village straggles along a lane off the A36 on the north-eastern fringes of the New Forest. This is East Wellow and the church here is dedicated to St Margaret, but it is not the saint herself whose phantom walks here, but another lady who many thought was close to being a saint herself. Wellow was the childhood home of Florence Nightingale and it was to the Church of St Margaret that she came with her family to worship.

It was from Wellow that Florence Nightingale left in 1854 to go to the British military hospital in Scutari, Turkey, where British casualties of the Crimean War were being cared for. Or rather, where they weren't being cared for. As a trained nurse, Nightingale was appalled by the lack of hygiene and nursing care being given to the wounded and sick soldiers. Backed up by a team of equally dedicated ladies, Nightingale cleaned out the wards and operating theatres with disinfectant, ensured all bandages and bed linen was thoroughly cleaned and spent long hours caring for the sick. She became famous as 'The Lady with the Lamp', as she ended her long days touring the wards with a lamp to check on the soldiers.

When she arrived the death rate at Scutari was 42 per cent. When she left it was 2 per cent.

Returning to England, Nightingale became a national heroine. The soldiers and their families worshipped her for her gentle care, the medical authorities applauded her for her scientific approach and common sense. She spent the rest of her life dedicated to establishing nursing schools, upgrading hospitals and to the improvement of health in Britain and the Empire. One of her early triumphs was the nursing school attached to St Thomas's Hospital in London, from where thousands of nurses, trained in the Nightingale methods, went out to save lives.

No matter how busy she was, Florence Nightingale always tried to get down to Wellow for a few days' rest whenever she could. When she died in 1910, the Nightingale family was offered the chance to bury Florence in Westminster Abbey as befits a national heroine. But Florence had left strict instructions that she was to be interred at Wellow in the grounds of the church where she had worshipped God and found her inspiration. And she lies there still.

Soon after her death, the shade of Florence Nightingale was seen on numerous occasions, sitting quietly in a pew in the church or walking slowly around the churchyard. And well she might, for this is a most beautiful little church dating from the 1240s and full of fascinating paintings and other details. I recommend that when you visit you should drop some money into the box for the church repair fund. I have rarely found a more deserving cause.

Florence Nightingale is a most busy ghost, for she is seen not only in Wellow, but also in the corridors of St Thomas's Hospital. A friend of mine, who trained as a nurse there some years ago, saw her once:

> She was dressed in an old-fashioned grey dress down to the ground. She came round the corner from the corridor into the ward and looked about. Then she walked out again. I was only a student nurse at the time and was all alone on night duty. There was not meant to be anyone else about apart from me and the Sister that came to check up from time to time. I wondered who this lady was and followed her out to the corridor, but she had vanished. I was told by older staff that this was the ghost of Florence Nightingale.

The funeral monument in the churchyard at East Wellow stands over the grave of Florence Nightingale, whose ghost haunts the area.

Florence Nightingale tends to the wounded of the Crimean War in a mid-Victorian engraving.

The second ghost of East Wellow has no name and nobody is very certain how often it appears. It is a phantom coach and four which trots down the lanes on occasion. One local chap told me that the coach is seen only at night. Another that it has not been seen for donkey's years. Neither had actually seen it and I could find nobody who had.

The little village of Breamore lies off the A338 about three miles north of Fordingbridge, right on the western edge of the New Forest. It is a straggling village, the tile-hung cottages being strung out around a great open space known as The Marsh. More of a large village green than a wetland, The Marsh has been the centre of village life for centuries.

It was here in 1163 that King Henry II first fell out with the Archbishop of Canterbury, St Thomas a Becket. King Henry had been engaged in a long-running dispute with the Church which had dragged on for years and become increasingly bitter. The details are complex, but they revolved around ancient rights to tax Church lands and impose English laws on clergy that had been enjoyed since time immemorial by the kings of England. But since these rights were not written down anywhere, the Popes were insisting that they did not exist. They refused to pay royal taxes or to obey royal laws.

When the old archbishop died, Henry appointed his friend Thomas a Becket to be the new Archbishop of Canterbury in the hope that his friend would ease tensions between Church and Crown, and so resolve the dispute. The King and Archbishop were riding through Breamore one day a few months after Thomas had become archbishop. They were on their way to inspect a nearby Augustinian Priory that had been founded in 1130. The priory was,

Breamore Church, scene of an historic argument between King Henry II and Archbishop Thomas à Becket.

at the time, the wealthiest monastery in Hampshire, and had spent some of its money on upgrading the parish church.

The pair stopped here to look at the work. Henry remarked that once the priory was paying its taxes it would be the king who decided where the money was spent. Thomas replied that the priory would not be paying its taxes, and that the money belonged to God's Church, not to the King. Henry was furious, and the rest of the visit was conducted in a frosty silence. The dispute led to tragedy. In 1170 four knights murdered Becket, thinking that they would gain Henry's favour by doing so. All they ensured was that all Christendom turned against Henry, who was forced to give way and promise to surrender his rights – though as a wily old lawyer himself he carefully avoided giving away very much at all. Disputes between the English Crown and the Catholic Church would continue until the sixteenth century, when King Henry VIII solved the matter once and for all when he made himself head of the Church in England and told the Popes to mind their own business.

In 1536 the priory was closed down on orders of King Henry VIII, as were so many other religious houses, and the monks given a modest pension on which to survive. The prior, Peter Finch, went on to become a bishop, though the lesser brothers faded from history.

They have not, however, faded from Breamore. In the churchyard of Breamore Church lie three stone coffins. These were excavated from the adjacent site of the priory in 1898 and placed here for safekeeping. It would seem that they have brought with them some spectral monks. As dusk comes down over the valley of the Avon, one or two grey spectral figures will appear near the yew tree beneath which the coffins rest. The hooded figures then drift off slowly towards the mysterious mizmaze that lies in a clump of trees not far away. Once there the figures slowly dissipate and vanish.

This mizmaze is a peculiar and mysterious object. It is a path carved into the turf that forms an intricate circular pattern some 90ft in diameter. Nor is this a maze in which the visitor can get lost, for there is just one path in and out again. It is not entirely clear how old this mizmaze might be. Some similar structures elsewhere in England date back to pre-Christian times, possibly as long ago as the building of Stonehenge and similar stone structures. It is known that the mizmaze at Breamore was here when the priory was built and that the monks soon found a use for it.

Pilgrims and sinners were encouraged to walk on their knees along the path until they reached the centre. There they had to pray for forgiveness, before crawling back out again. Salvation was thus assured. Whether or not the phantom monks from the churchyard have come here to seek salvation is unclear. But other ghosts most certainly do. Shadowy figures have been seen shuffling along the path, and the groans, prayers and entreaties of these medieval pilgrims still drift across the mizmaze on occasion.

Within a short distance of the church and maze stands Breamore House. The house was built in 1583 by the Dodington family, a notable Hampshire dynasty of squires and landowners. It has remained remarkably unaltered since, and today offers visitors a clear idea of what one of England's grander manor houses was like at the time of the Spanish Armada.

In 1660 the Breamore estate was given as a dowry to young Lady Anne Dodington when she married Sir Robert Greville, Lord Brooke. Sixty years later the estate was sold to Sir Edward Hulse, the Royal Physician. Hulse had remarkable tact, being able to survive in his post through the turbulent years that saw Queen Anne pass away and replaced by King George I and then George II. The Hulse family own the house still.

The haunting is connected to Lady Anne's mother and grandmother. The phantom of the elder Mrs Dodington met with tragedy in 1600 when her husband, William, killed himself in London by throwing himself from the steeple of St Sepulchre's Church when a lawsuit went against him. Poor Mrs Dodington had a portrait of herself painted in mourning clothes, placed it in the house and then faded away. Three years later her son, another William, was knighted. His wife, the younger Mrs Dodington, was murdered in 1630 by her own son in a deranged fit.

The younger Mrs Dodington haunts the Blue Bedroom, the chamber in which she was killed. She is said to bring tragedy in her wake. The appearance of the ghost presages serious illness or death for the owners of the house. Even more disturbing is the phantom of the older Mrs Dodington. Her portrait hangs in the house as it has done since it was put there on the orders of the subject herself. As she lay dying, Mrs Dodington cursed her luck and promised that equally dire fortune would haunt whoever moved her portrait. Over the years few people have risked the wrath of Mrs Dodington by moving the portrait. When Sir Edward Hulse bought the house it was on the condition that the portrait remain in the house forever. His descendants leave it there still. One man did move it in the 1950s when cleaning the house, but later that day had a fall and broke his leg. Nobody has touched it since.

The house now plays host to an agricultural museum as well as the more usual attractions of a stately home. Visitors can see full-size replicas of a farm worker's cottage before the advent of electricity, a blacksmith's shop, a dairy, wheelwright's shop, a brewery, a saddler's shop and cobbler's shed. The village shop, school, cooperage, bakers, laundry and early garage represent recent developments.

The village of Setley lies off the A337 in a remote area of the southern New Forest. Back in the early nineteenth century a wealthy gentleman was travelling down to Lymington when he was set upon by three unemployed sailors a short distance north of here. The man was brutally murdered and his body stripped of everything of value, then tossed into the River Boldre. The sailors decided to get as far away as possible, but first stopped at the Filly Inn in Setley for some refreshments.

Unfortunately for them, the landlord recognised them as the same penniless trio who had been hanging around the area for the past few days. And yet here they were, suddenly flush with money and owning a heavy gold watch and other fine clothes and jewellery. Deeply suspicious

At the heart of the New Forest stands the Rufus Stone, scene of a mysterious death that led to a persistent haunting.

of how these tough characters had come by their sudden wealth, the landlord sent his potboy running to Lyndhurst to summon the forces of law and order.

The three killers were still drinking when the magistrate's men arrived to question them. Unable to come up with a convincing story to account for their sudden wealth, the men were put in custody while investigations were undertaken. A few days later the dead man's body was discovered and all became clear. The three sailors were hanged from a gibbet beside what is now the A337, a mile north of the pub. Their bodies were left to swing as a grisly reminder to others of what awaited criminals in the area.

After the bodies were taken down and disposed of in a pauper's grave, the ghosts began to walk. The phantoms of the three sailors began to be seen walking from the gibbet to the pub. The grim execution tree has long since rotted away, but the ghosts remain. If you take yourself down to Setley, you might see them walking with bowed heads along the main road toward the pub where they were arrested.

The pub itself has also experienced some odd happenings. The focus for the activity is the main bar, where glasses have been seen to move of their own accord. Upstairs, the corridor and one of the bedrooms has played host to a vague and ill-defined figure that flits away out of sight as soon as it is seen.

Another wayside killing led to a rather different haunting. In 1815 the Duke of Wellington won a convincing victory over the French Emperor Napoleon I at Waterloo in present-day Belgium. It was important that the news of the victory reach London as quickly as possible, so a number of couriers were sent to follow different routes in case bad weather or other mishaps held up the news. One such was an army officer who landed at Poole, and was spurring toward London when he was set upon by person or persons unknown in what is now Alma Lane, Hale. The poor man was murdered and his pockets emptied. Nobody was ever caught for the crime, which may explain why the victim's ghost is still seen now and then in the lane.

WILLIAM II., SURNAMED RUFUS.

William Rufus ruled England from 1087 to 1100. His reign has proved to be as controversial among modern historians as it was at the time. This Victorian engraving is taken from a portrait of the king on one of his coins.

At the heart of the New Forest stands the Rufus Stone. It lies in the area of the New Forest known as Stricknage Woods, off the A31, about nine miles east of Ringwood and well signposted. There is a small car park thoughtfully provided by the Forestry Commission. In anything but the driest weather, bring some wellington boots as the ground in this area can be quite marshy. On warm summer evenings a short, stocky man with flame-red hair may be seen here. He wears a golden tunic and stout boots. The man wanders moodily around the clearing ignoring anyone who may be present. After a few minutes the man turns and walks slowly off to the west along a little-used path between the trees. He speaks to nobody, looks at nobody. In truth, he has little need to do so.

This is the ghost of a king.

The centre of the haunting is the Rufus Stone. The stone weathered away many years ago and now a metal obelisk marks the site of a 900-year-old killing. And, as with many hauntings, the ghost of the victim may walk because the murderer was never brought to justice. But there is no real mystery as to the man behind the crime, at least not now.

King William II of England was nicknamed Rufus for his red hair and ruddy complexion. He was, most people agree, a greedy, corrupt debauchee who stooped to just about every vice known to medieval man – and to a few that he invented himself. On the plus side, however, he was a good law-maker who energetically led English armies to victory over the French, Welsh and Scots in turn.

In the summer of 1100 he had been on the throne for thirteen years. His elder brother, Robert, Duke of Normandy, was off in the Crusades and his younger brother, Henry, was enjoying a comfortable life on the revenues of his estates. On 2 August William set off to hunt deer in the New Forest with a group of friends and Henry with no thought of coming disaster.

Just before dusk one of the hunters, a Norman knight named Sir Walter Tyrrell, shot an arrow at a galloping stag but the arrow glanced off and disappeared into a thicket. Pushing through the bushes to find his arrow, Tyrrell was shocked to see the King lying dead with an arrow in his chest. Hearing young Henry and the others approaching, Tyrrell was suddenly frightened of what they would do to him if they thought that he had killed the King on purpose. He leapt on his horse and galloped off, not stopping until he reached the safety of his estates in Normandy. The King's brother, when he saw the corpse, also leapt to the saddle and galloped off. He rode straight to Winchester to announce what had happened and put a strong guard of men loyal to himself on the Royal Treasury.

As for the other knights out on the hunt, they hurriedly ordered a pair of peasants to put the King's body on a cart and take it to Winchester. Then they galloped off at top speed. Arriving at Winchester, they produced a huntsman who said he had seen Tyrrell's arrow hit the King. There was nothing he could do, said the tearful man, to save the King.

It was all very sad, but that did not stop young Henry organising a hurried coronation so that he was safely on the throne before his elder brother could get back from the Crusades to interfere.

On the other side of the Channel, however, Tyrrell was having time for quiet reflection. He decided that he could not have killed the King. His arrow had glanced off the stag's back, then entered thick bushes. It would not have had enough power to plunge as deeply into the King's chest as did the fatal arrow. Anyway, he thought, the King had been alone when Tyrrell arrived. Where was the huntsman who was meant to be escorting the King, and who claimed to have seen the fatal arrow strike home?

If Tyrrell was innocent of accidental killing, who really had killed the King? Only one man had gained from the death: the brother who became King Henry I. And he had been suspiciously well-prepared to take the throne immediately afterwards.

It is probably because his own brother killed him – and escaped retribution – that the ghost of King William II returns to the New Forest on the anniversary of his death. The peasants who loaded the King's body on to a cart reported that it was still dripping blood as it was jolted along to Winchester. In all likelihood the King was still alive. The King's ghost is said to walk off towards Winchester along those same forest tracks.

I came to the Rufus Stone on a bright day in August to see the site of the killing and the haunting. Visitors milled around the obelisk, birds chattered overhead and squirrels scampered through the leaves. As the sun slipped down behind the trees west of the Rufus Stone, the gloom of dusk settled over the now silent forest. Nothing moved, and no ghost came.

In hindsight it was not terribly surprising. King William was killed on 2 August, but the calendar has been changed since then. In the modern calendar it is 22 July that is the anniversary of the killing. It looks like I must return once more to that clearing in the New Forest and wait for the sun to set.

After exploring the haunted area, you can continue down the single-track road to the aptly named Sir Walter Tyrrell pub.

The King's ghost is not the only spectral mark that the crime left in the New Forest. Another haunting is rather less well known, though the lane where it takes place has been named for the ghost. Tyrell's Lane lies off the road leading into Burley Street from the village of Burley proper. Its gravel surface runs off into the woods of the New Forest and, to make finding it even easier, it has a nameplate attached to sturdy concrete pillars.

This is the route that Walter Tyrrell took after the fatal arrow was shot. He was trying to escape the King's retainers. He galloped down this lane and his ghost still does. Tyrrell took ship at Poole as he fled to France, so his route would have brought him this way. If Tyrrell's ghost does gallop through Burley, this would make sense. Tyrrell would have been in fear of his life at the

The shop in Burley that is haunted by a ghostly cat, which can be very friendly to visiting tourists.

Burley's Queens Head Hotel was the venue for some very unnerving moaning, but the haunting ceased after a hidden chamber was discovered.

The lonely lane across heath land east of Burley is the haunt of a phantom highwayman.

time. Strong emotions such as that seem to create ghosts and hauntings. I wandered down the gravel lane. There was no ghost to be seen and everything seemed quiet. But then it would, for this is a ghost that moves in silence.

The village of Burley lies on the western fringes of the New Forest between the A31 and A35. Although the lanes that lead to the village are unnumbered, the village is well signposted. New Forest ponies wander the streets of Burley seemingly oblivious to the traffic and visitors that throng this popular village in the summer season. The ghosts are similarly tolerant of the passing tourists, one of them seems to relish the company.

It is the ghostly cat which likes the tourists best. It will appear in front of them, purring with pleasure and, sometimes, rubbing up against them just as a living cat would do. The grey cat has its home in the quaint knick-knack shop known as the Coven of Witches. The owner, Jenny Tucker, told me about it when I called in at the village:

It's a funny thing. We didn't have any sign of the ghostly cat when we first bought the shop. There was nothing unusual at all. Then all of a sudden this cat started turning up. It looked just like a real cat, and it was only when we realised that it was appearing and disappearing that it occurred to us that it was a phantom. It was my friend from the art shop down the road who pointed something out to me. When we bought the shop there was this large china cat in the window. The phantom cat started appearing only after we got rid of the china cat. Odd, isn't it?

These days we hardly pay it any attention at all. It will sit there watching the people in the shop quite happily. Or it will walk behind the counter, brushing up against the back of my legs as it passes. I think it might have something to do with the ley line that runs through this shop. There is certainly tremendous atmosphere and energy here. You can really feel it sometimes.

Across the way from the Coven of Witches stands the imposing Queens Head Hotel. Parts of the pub date back to 1660. This was the heyday of the smugglers in the New Forest, and Burley was a major centre for the nefarious trade. Small ships laden with French brandy and other

The woods of Castle Hill in the New Forest were once the home to a dragon, complete with fire-breathing ferocity and scaly ugliness.

goods would land at night near Christchurch Bay and their cargos would be taken by pack horse through the narrow paths of the New Forest to be stored at farmhouses or barns before being taken onwards to the markets of England.

The Queens Head had a long-held reputation for being involved in the business. One night in the later seventeenth century the excise men came calling and confiscated an impressive £238 worth of illegal imports. Thereafter, the excise men were never again able to find anything illegal at the Queens Head, though the inn remained a well-known haunt of the smugglers. When import duties were lowered in the early nineteenth century, smuggling became less profitable and so the smugglers ceased trading.

By the later nineteenth century the Queens Head was famous for quite a different reason. There was something in the bar – or rather underneath it. On moonlit nights – the nights favoured by the old-time smugglers – there was often a clearly audible moaning or whining heard emanating from underground. So regular did the noises become that they were a bit of a tourist attraction in their own right. Then, in the 1950s, renovation work was done that uncovered a long-hidden hatchway. The hatch gave on to a short tunnel which led to a vaulted chamber beneath the bar area. The origin of the ghostly moans was revealed, but there was no hidden skeleton of anyone who had died there moaning. More likely this chamber was the place where the smugglers hid their goods from prying excise men. Once the chamber was uncovered the moaning ceased and is not heard today.

I had also heard talk of a phantom highwayman up on the heathland east of the village around the place known as Durhurst Cross. Nobody in the village seemed to know much about him, however. Perhaps he has not been seen recently.

Another ghost is reported to lurk in Burley Lawn. He is said to be seen riding past the tree where he was hanged back in 1759. He rides a brown horse and wears a smart suit with bright metal buttons. You cannot miss him if he rides, the story goes. No doubt this is true. I made my way to Burley Lawn, but there was no sign of which tree might be the haunted one. I asked a passer-by about the ghost.

The ghostly dragon of Burley's Castle Hill has been seen in recent years flying over the woods that line the lane to the hilltop.

'Now, I have heard of that story,' said a gentleman in a thick tweed jacket. He looked around and rubbed his chin. 'Don't know exactly where he is meant to be seen. But it is definitely round here. They hanged him here, you see.'

Next on the list was a more enigmatic apparition. This was no less than a dragon, complete with fire-breathing ferocity and scaly ugliness. Back in the thirteenth century, this beast flew down from lands unknown and made his lair on Castle Hill. At first, the dragon ate whatever came to hand, including a couple of villagers. But the good folk of Burley soon found that if they tied a sheep on Beacon Hill, the dragon would eat that whenever he was hungry and leave the villagers alone. After some months, the man whose turn it was to sacrifice one of his sheep put out a bowl of milk instead, in the hope of getting off lightly. This angered the dragon which went on the rampage, killing everything and everyone in its path.

Fortunately, a knight was passing and, having prayed for divine assistance in Burley Church, he dispatched the dragon after a titanic struggle. It is said that the dragon's ghost still flies from Castle Hill to Beacon Hill on clear nights when a full moon bathes the New Forest in its pale, phantom light, although to be honest I could find nobody who had seen the thing.

The last of the Burley ghosts is the one seen most often, and the saddest. This is the ghost of a little boy in ragged clothes. He is seen walking along the lanes around Burley weeping bitterly and plucking at his threadbare, tattered clothes. This hapless boy was murdered by his own father back in the eighteenth century, apparently in a fit of temper, though some say because the father resented the cost of bringing up a child when he could spend his money on drink. Whatever the cause, the boy was killed and his unhappy spirit lurks around Burley to this day. Perhaps one day he will find the peace he deserves.

At Burgate, near Fordingbridge, stands the Tudor Rose Inn. When I called there in 2003 the manager, Jan Haggart, was not about. However, I left my card and a request for information. She wrote to me a few days later:

The White Hart at Ringwood stands in the Market Place, the ancient heart of the town.

I have only taken over the management of this site three weeks ago, and therefore have no definite proof of ghostly goings on but this is what I know. The building dates back to 14th century when it was then two cottages. It has since served as a private dwelling, a coaching station (around the turn of the 20th century), a French styled restaurant (1960s) before being extended and renamed in the early 1970s.

The central fireplace area dates back to 14th century and where practical has been preserved. Also preserved is the cavalier ghost and those who have previously resided in these rooms will claim his existence. His most annoying habit is to knock courteously on the door before entering and then slam it violently behind him, for this reason and to ensure the comfort of our guests, we have removed as many of the doors as possible.

Another fine place to dine that is haunted is the White Hart at Ringwood. Ringwood lies astride the A31 on the western edge of the New Forest. The main road bypasses the old town centre, as does the B3347 which branches off south towards Christchurch. The Original White Hart stands in the Market Place, the ancient heart of Ringwood.

Dee Wade, the landlady of the Original White Hart in Ringwood, was cautious about her resident phantom. 'I've not seen her myself,' Dee said. 'But I've only been landlady for three months. I can only tell you what others have told me. It's hearsay really.'

It turned out to be most impressive hearsay.

I had only dropped in for a bite to eat before investigating a couple of other ghosts in Ringwood and had not been expecting to find a ghost at all. But the barmaid had put me right and called Dee over to explain things. She began:

Now the only thing that I've experienced myself is the back door over there. In the summer we prop it open, but it keeps closing itself. Could be the wind, I suppose, but it never does it when you

The stairs that lead from the reception area to the function room at the White Hart in Ringwood. This staircase is the spot where the ghostly lady of the pub has been seen most often in recent years.

are here to see it. But turn your back and it shuts. Doesn't matter what you prop it open with – a chair, a brick, whatever. It just keeps shutting.

Anyway, they tell me that our ghost is of an old chambermaid or something. She hangs about towards the back of the hotel, near the kitchens. See those stairs? That's where she is seen most often. A lady in a grey dress, I'm told. And in the function room beyond. Well, we had all sorts of trouble back there. Before my time, mind.

Well it was being all refurbished you see. To be a restaurant or function room. Anyway, our phantom chambermaid was obsessed with keeping things tidy. She does that, you see. Tidies things up. So she kept putting tools back in boxes when the workmen weren't looking. Like she shuts the back door when you are not looking. It got so bad that the men refused to work in there alone. There always had to be three of them at a time.

Dee shook her head.

'You'd best come through to the kitchen,' Dee said. I followed her up the haunted stairs and through the function room to the kitchens. 'She is very active in here,' she confided. 'Moving stuff about and so on. They do tell me, anyway. Odd, really. This is one of the newest parts of the building. I can understand those stairs, they are very old. Part of the original inn. But out here?' Dee shrugged.

'I'm told we had an exorcism here back in the 1960s,' she continued. 'You can see the cross they carved in the wall by the stairs.' Had it done any good? Dee shrugged again. 'Can't say. Maybe she was more active before, but she is still about. Well, so I am told.'

The kitchen at the White Hart at Ringwood has been the scene of assorted paranormal events and hauntings.

But if Dee was cautious about her pub's spectral resident, she was most definite about the pub's history.

This is the Original White Hart, see. All the other White Hart pubs around just copied our name. It was hundreds of years ago when the King, Queen and the knights and so on were out hunting in the New Forest. They spotted this pure white deer and gave chase. Well the deer led them a good race, gave them great sport it did. Finally they got it cornered, and the deer turned out to be so tame and gentle it went up and nuzzled the Queen. And she persuaded the King not to kill it. Instead they put a golden collar round its neck and made it a pet. The first place they came to was Ringwood, you see, and they stopped here for a meal. So the King said the name of the inn had to be changed to The White Hart. That is how we got our name. Oh yes, all the others just copied us. I've been meaning to look that story up more properly like. You know, for history. But that's how we got our name. That's why the sign outside says Original White Hart.

I thanked Dee for her hospitality and her ghost story. I went back outside and looked up at the pub sign. The Original, indeed.

Anyway, it was then time to set off to investigate the ghosts that had actually brought me to Ringwood. A pair of ghosts which had been quiet for some years have, it seems, suddenly put

The narrow Ebenezer Lane has been the site of a periodic haunting by a ghostly man and woman for some decades.

The lovely church at Boldre is rather remote, being located some distance from the village itself.

in an appearance. Or rather, one of them has. The tiny Ebenezer Lane became quite famous in the 1960s when a phantom lady and gentleman dating from the time the houses were built, in the 1750s, suddenly became a lot more active. The ghosts had been around for some time, but for an unexplained reason they were seen quite often during the summer months of 1967. The ghosts were no great bother, of course. They just seemed to like it in Ebenezer Lane and stood around chatting to each other.

That was years ago, and the ghosts had not been seen much in the intervening years. Not until autumn 2003, that is. A lady who lives nearby saw the ghost of a man in eighteenth century dress one day. At the time she thought little of it. After all, she reasoned, he might be someone in fancy dress, although even then she did think there was something odd about the man. A few weeks later she saw him again. This time she took more interest and watched as the man walked into Ebenezer Lane. She followed quickly, turning the corner only seconds after the man had done. But he was gone. Which was when she contacted me.

The first task after leaving the Original White Hart was to find Ebenezer Lane, which was not easy. The lady who called said it was off Christchurch Road, but I walked up and down without seeing it. Only after asking a helpful lady in a newsagent's shop, was I directed to a narrow alley beside a chip shop. The lane in question was quiet enough, and nobody was about.

The chip shop, however, was open. I asked the man doing the frying if he knew anything about the ghosts. He didn't, but a customer just leaving did.

'Oh yes, some years back wasn't it. A man and woman in old-fashioned clothes were seen quite a few times.' I asked if she knew the ghosts were back. 'I did hear that someone had seen something, but I can't say I know any details.'

It seems the phantom man is back. Where his lady might be is unknown.

The other ghost that had brought me to Ringwood was a grey lady, said to haunt the Market Place. This unfortunate lady was run down and killed by a truck some time before the Second World War. It seems that she is seen most often in the later afternoon, though it is unclear why this should be the case.

The lane at Boldre along which the ghostly knight rides before dismounting to enter the church and kneel in prayer.

The phantom knight of Boldre, as described to the author by an eyewitness. The armorial bearings are conjectural.

Walking back up Christchurch Road, I found the Market Place easily enough. It was bustling with people. I tried a couple of shops, but at first nobody knew about the ghost. Not until I had almost given up did I find somebody who knew of the phantom.

'Oh yes,' a man who had just parked his car responded. 'My Dad used to go on about her. He said that she used to hang around near a restaurant called the Four Seasons, frightened the staff a fair bit and got in the newspapers. Not heard much recently, it must be said.'

And that was that. The phantoms of Ringwood seem to be a fleeting lot. They come and go, but they don't stay around for long. Very different was the ghost of Boldre, which was where I was off to next.

Honour, rebellion and bloodshed lie behind the haunting of Boldre Church, though the violence lies far in the past and the church is now a gentle, relaxing place. The Church of St John may be the parish church of Boldre, but it is not in the village itself. To find the church follow the road signs off the A337 to Boldre. Once in the village, other signs show the way to the church. These lead down a narrow, tree-lined lane that runs for well over a mile through woods and fields before it turns sharp right. Suddenly the trees fall away and the church lies in front of you. There is a car park just beyond the church, and it is advisable to use this as otherwise your car might block the lane.

Back in 1215 Sir William de Vernun owned vast estates to the west of the New Forest, and Boldre was just one of his many manors. Vernun was a tough, hard man but he had a reputation for fairness. When King John ruled with astonishing arrogance and little regard for the law, the fairness in Sir William made him view the King with distaste. He joined the rebellious nobles who resisted the worst excesses of John's dictatorial rule. Eventually the barons dragged John to Runneymede where they forced him to sign the Magna Carta, a document that was to form the bedrock of the rights and liberties of the English. Sir William was among those who donned his armour and forced King John to sign.

After all the excitement, Vernun returned to his estates hoping to enjoy a peaceful life and better government. Along with many others he was disappointed. John was soon up to his old tricks again, so again the nobles gathered together. Vernun donned his armour and rode off to join them. This time the barons announced that John was unfit to be King and declared that England wanted a new King. They chose Louis, son of King Philip of France. Louis landed in England, promising to obey the Magna Carta and to rule with justice. Sir William brought Louis to his estates and to Boldre Church. A stained-glass panel was put in the large west window to mark the event, and was decorated with the fleur-de-lys of France.

Then, in September 1216, King John died. He left a nine-year-old heir as Henry III and put the ageing nobleman Sir William Marshall in charge as regent. Everyone in England knew and respected Sir William Marshall, including Vernun. When Marshall promised fair laws and good government, he was believed. The rebellion collapsed and Louis fled back to France. Vernun returned to his estates around Boldre and lived in peace until his death.

But the peace of Boldre was soon to be disturbed. It was not long before a ghostly knight in armour began riding up to the church, followed by a retinue of armed men. Clanking noisily, the group marched into the church and up to the altar. There they knelt in prayer before vanishing. What could it mean? The villagers did not know, but they recognised the knight – it was Sir William de Vernun.

The phantom knight rides up to Boldre Church to this day. His retinue of armed men is now reduced to a pair of archers, for the other phantoms seem to have faded with the centuries. Sir William is seen most often riding up the lane to the church and into the churchyard. The archers have been glimpsed kneeling in front of the altar.

I came to Boldre on a bright, sunny afternoon after my trip to Ringwood. There was nobody about to ask for news of the phantom knight, but there was much else to do. There was the sunshine to be enjoyed, for a start, while in the church is a moving tribute to the men of HMS *Hood* who died in the cold North Atlantic fighting the German battleship *Bismarck* in 1941. And St John the Baptist is a charming rural church in its own right. The stained glass is impressive and parts of the stonework were erected in 1080. Actually, it is thought that the original church embraced a stone circle dating back to around 2,000 BC. This would seem to have been a place of worship for over 4,000 years.

It is a double tragedy that lies behind the haunting of the Wagon and Horses pub at Walhampton, across the estuary from Lymington. Back in 1893 the body of local farmer was found lying in nearby fields. He had been shot dead with a single blast in the back from his own shotgun, which lay nearby. Naturally, foul play was suspected, but the hapless farmer did not seem to have any enemies, was clear of debt and there was no obvious suspect or motives.

Then Walhampton gamekeeper Henry Card came forward with a theory. He stated that the farmer had accidentally shot himself in the back. Card said that it was relatively easy for this to happen if a man were in the custom of carrying a shotgun in a particular way, then tripped and fell in such fashion as to jar the gun suddenly. He offered to put on a demonstration for sceptical police and others at the Wagon and Horses. On the appointed day, Card appeared with his own shotgun and proceeded to show how he thought the mishap had occurred. Tragically for him,

The friendly pub at Walhampton was the scene of a tragic accident that has led to the haunting.

his own gun was not unloaded as he clearly believed. The demonstration went only too well and Card shot himself in exactly the manner the farmer had done. He died instantly.

For decades after that fatal day the ghost of Henry Card was encountered in the bar of the Wagon and Horses. He was most often seen standing, staring out of the window. After the 1950s the phantom was seen less often and today the ghost is rarely if ever seen. It is, however, blamed for any keys or other objects that go missing.

Over the estuary lies Lymington which has perhaps the most haunted pub in the county, certainly in the New Forest. The Angel claims to be the haunt of no fewer than four ghosts. The first and apparently most active is a coachman from the early nineteenth century. He is seen from the bar, but never in it. Instead he is seen peering in through the window from the yard. He wears a heavy cloak with a cape about his shoulders drawn up tight as if against bitter winter weather, and has a hat pulled down firmly about his ears. The second phantom is a sailor in a reefer jacket with brass buttons. He is not seen so often, and then only late at night. The third spectre is a little girl with fair hair who skips about the second floor. The final phantom takes the form of spectral piano music that is heard downstairs.

THE SOUTH EAST

The great ports of Portsmouth and Southampton with their adjacent suburbs and linked towns dominate the coastline in the eastern part of the county. Of the two, Southampton is the older, having been a port back in Roman times. In 1016 King Canute was here when flattering courtiers told him that he was so powerful even the tides would obey him. He led them down to the beach and got his feet wet, proving them wrong. Crusaders setting out in the Middle Ages to fight the Moslems in the Holy Land embarked from here, and in 1620 the *Mayflower* set off for America from here. By contrast, Portsmouth is almost a new town. It emerged as a port only in the 1190s, but from the start was a military base. The massive rebuilding of the naval docks that ensured Portsmouth's prosperity began in the 1660s and at their peak they covered over 300 acres.

Unfortunately, both towns suffered very badly from German bombs during the Second World War. Large areas were flattened, to be replaced in the post-war years by modern buildings. Sadly, among those that went were some of the most haunted structures in the county.

Despite the best efforts of the Luftwaffe, some ancient haunted buildings remain, and of these the White Swan in Portsmouth is probably the most actively haunted. The phantom here is of a serving maid employed in the inn during the Victorian period. She was married to a sailor, but does not seem to have been particularly faithful to him during his long voyages in the service of Her Majesty. She is alleged to have bestowed her favours on a well-to-do local tradesman who plied her with gifts of jewellery and other temptations. At least, that is what the sailor was told on his return from one voyage, and he was convinced by whatever evidence he was given.

Striding round to the White Swan, the sailor surprised his wife at work and confronted her with the allegations. A vicious quarrel followed, during which the sailor whipped out his splicing knife and slit his wife's throat. The landlord and customers pounced on the sailor, holding him prisoner until the police could arrive and haul the man off to the inevitable trial and execution that followed.

The ghost that returns to the White Swan is that of the murdered serving maid. She appears dressed in a white or cream dress, which is unusual as she would have worked in a darker coloured gown. Perhaps she is trying to make a point by wearing virginal white. She continues to be seen more than a century after her demise, flitting about near the fireplace in the main bar, which according to tradition is the spot where she died.

The old naval harbour at Portsmouth is famous for HMS *Victory*, which is preserved here in dry dock, and the other ships and exhibits that make this a major tourist attraction. Rather less known is the ghostly man who potters about near Blockhouse Point. This is one of the very few ghosts that is said to rattle chains, something of a cliché in movies and books but remarkably rare in real spooks.

This is the spectre of Jack the Painter, who was hanged here in 1776 from the yardarm of the warship HMS *Arethusa*. His crime was to have started a fire in the rope house, then a capital offence due to the immense amount of damage to the nation's war effort that could result from a fire in a naval dockyard filled with wooden ships and inflammable materials. Why Jack should have chosen to start the fire is not recorded, but there seems to have been no doubt as to his guilt.

Warships ride at anchor off Portsmouth at the time of Jack the Painter, who was hanged here in 1776.

The body was hung in chains as a grim warning to others tempted to repeat the crime. In this instance the warning did not work. Jack the Painter's fellow workers cut down the skeleton and sold the bones as souvenirs or pawned them to raise money. This led to a little ditty that did the rounds in Portsmouth at the time:

> Whose bones, some years since taken down,
> Were bought in curious way to town
> And left in pledge for half a crown?
> Why truly, Jack the Painter.

The ghost has also been seen around the site of the gibbet where he died.

The Theatre Royal has long been rumoured to be haunted, and by a number of ghosts. The oldest, but not the most active in recent years, is that of the founder, Henry Rutley. That Mr Rutley is still around in phantom form is quite remarkable, for his theatre has had a very chequered career.

It was in 1856 that Henry Rutley bought Landport Hall, then a racquet court, and announced that he would be turning it into a theatre. The local magistrates were not terribly impressed by Rutley's past career as a circus owner and imposed strict conditions before they granted a license. Rutley had said that the new theatre would be 'a place of entertainment to which the middle classes of the borough might resort.' He was as good as his word, staging operas, dramas, comedies and melodramas with quality casts and great appeal to the middle classes.

The ghostly monk of Netley, from an old engraving.

The South Front of Netley Abbey. This frontage is made up mostly of the domestic buildings, which were readily converted to a house after the abbey was closed down by order of King Henry VIII in the 1540s.

The nave of the church at Netley Abbey. The ghostly monk is seen most often in this part of the ruins.

Fears that the theatre would turn out to be a music hall for the beer-swilling masses were misplaced, no doubt much to the annoyance of some.

Rutley died in 1874, and the theatre passed into the hands of John Boughton, who rebuilt and renovated the place to make it what it is today. In 1932 the theatre became a cinema and it closed completely in 1968. The structure stood empty for years, but in 2004 money was found to renovate the structure completely and return it to its Victorian splendour, though with modern amenities.

The second ghost is even less active, not having been seen for many years. This is the phantom of an actor who committed suicide by slitting his throat in his dressing room around 1895. For decades he haunted the room where he died, but this section of the theatre was pulled down and redeveloped during the long years of neglect and the ghost is now never seen. Some maintain that the unfortunate suicide victim was not an actor, but an accountant who had been fiddling the books to line his own pockets.

What is seen with some regularity is the ghostly soldier who sits in one of the boxes. If the box is empty for a show, the shadowy figure of the soldier is sometimes seen, both by cast members on-stage and by audience members in the stalls. At other times a particularly cold blast of air sweeps out of the box to engulf those walking down the stairs past the door that gives access to it. Those who have experienced it report that the blast of air is not only very cold and very sudden, but remarkably odd as well. It is usually put down to the ghostly soldier.

Who this phantom might be, nobody is entirely certain. His khaki uniform puts him firmly into the period before modern green uniforms, but opinion is divided as to whether he dates to the First or Second World War. No story is attached to him.

Standing on the coast between Portsmouth and Southampton is Netley, famous for its ruined abbey. Netley Abbey was founded in the thirteenth century as a branch of the larger religious house at Beaulieu. It was never particularly big, but was famed both for its elegant buildings and for its strict adherence to the Cistercian teachings. After the dissolution of the monasteries by King Henry VIII, the abbey was turned into a private house by William Paulet, Marquess of Winchester. By the eighteenth century the house was in disrepair and was bought by a local builder who planned to demolish it and use the stones for other buildings. On the very first day of demolition work, a hunk of stone tracery from a window fell on the builder and killed him. Taking this as an omen, the workmen halted demolition and the abbey buildings were left to moulder gently into ruin.

The ghost here is, unsurprisingly, that of a monk who paces quietly about the ruins of the monastic church. Rather less expected is the tale that he is guarding a hidden chamber that hides a terrible secret. What this secret might be, nobody is entirely certain. Back in the days when the abbey was a private house a gardener named Slown was digging when he uncovered an opening. He clambered down to investigate, only to emerge a few minutes later and to begin hurling clods of earth back down into the hole. 'Block it up!' he screamed. 'In the name of God, block it up!' He then collapsed in a faint. When he came to he was a broken man, remaining nervous and easily startled for the rest of his life. He never told what he had found, maintaining that he could remember nothing.

A short distance away stands the elegant, domed chapel that once belonged to a vast military hospital, since demolished. The hospital was haunted by a nurse, but she has not been reported in the chapel in recent years.

The city of Southampton can boast two very old and remarkably well-haunted pubs. The first is the imposing Dolphin Hotel in the High Street. This magnificent building has a grand Georgian facade of brick and stone with projecting bay windows, but this is a mere mask added by an eighteenth-century owner who wanted his hotel to look modern. The structure behind

The chapel of the former military hospital at Netley. The ghostly nurse has been glimpsed a few times in and around this building since the rest of the hospital was demolished.

the facade is considerably older, mostly of Tudor origins but with some fragments dating back around 900 years.

Bob Musker, the landlord in the autumn of 2008 when I called most recently, took me down to the medieval vaults that were excavated in about 1250. 'This area is haunted by two ghosts,' said Bob. 'An older man called Tom who we believe to have been a manual worker at the Dolphin – maybe a cellar man who looked after the barrels of wine, which would have been stored here throughout the centuries, when Southampton was famed for importing wines from our French neighbours. Sadly a young lad, who remains nameless, accompanies Tom – but we don't know much about him.'

We then went back up to the ground floor, a large section of which was gutted and rebuilt in the 1890s. 'This area is haunted by our most famous ghost,' declared Bob. 'Molly is the ghost that we know most about. Molly was a chamber maid and, as with many servants, she would have lived in the hotel. She fell in love and was spurned, tragically she took her own life in the old stable block. Molly has been seen by many people over the years, but a notable sighting was made by an American serviceman in the mid-1990s who saw her top half walk across his room – her lower half being below the floor's surface. Investigation showed that the new block which was built in 1890 was built on the site of an old stable block, which presumably had different floor levels – maybe he saw Molly walking to her death.'

I know that ghosts are traditionally meant to go floating through the air but in my experience they don't. The explanation here seems to be that Molly the maid worked here before the refurbishments took place. The floor level was then lower than it is now, so the ghost is walking where the floor was when Molly was alive. So far as she is concerned she is not walking through a solid wooden floor but actually on one.

Bob was keen to push on to the Assembly Rooms on the first floor, which were built in around 1750.

HENRY V.

King Henry V was in Southampton preparing for the campaign that would bring him immortal glory at the Battle of Agincourt, when the events at the Red Lion took place that are now recreated in spectral form.

This area is haunted by just one ghost, a portly gentleman in Georgian attire called Beau. Maybe Beau was attending one of the famous assemblies that were held at the Dolphin in the 1700s and early in the 1800s – without a doubt the most famous attendee was Jane Austen who danced here on her 18th Birthday. Beau is seen to gaze wistfully out of one of the large bay windows – you may even see him from the street if you look closely.

And up on the first floor corridor there is a grey lady who seems to date to around the 1890s. She certainly wears Victorian style clothes. This is our most seen ghost in recent times and as recently as June 2004 was seen and 'felt' by Kerry James, the hotel's marketing manager. Flowing dresses and ribbons – maybe she was staying before boarding one of the many ships that left our port in those days.

The other haunted hostelry in Southampton is the Red Lion. This charming pub looks older than the Dolphin, with its Tudor facade and ancient exposed beams within, but is in fact more modern. It was built in around 1350, some 200 years after the Dolphin was begun, but has not undergone a Georgian upgrade and so looks the older of the two. The hauntings here date back to a quite remarkable incident that took place in 1415.

King Henry V was then new to the throne of England, and he was not universally popular. Perhaps in an effort to gain popularity, he declared war on France and gathered an army and fleet in Southampton with which to invade the ancient enemy of England. One problem that Henry had was that he was not, in purely legal terms, the true king. His father, Henry IV, had usurped the crown from the incompetent Richard II, who was subsequently murdered. Although most Englishmen had been glad to see the end of Richard and the ascension of the famously efficient Henry IV, the true heir had been Richard's nephew, the Earl of March. When Henry IV grabbed the throne, March was barely out of nappies, but by 1415 he was a fully grown man who had proved himself courageous in war and competent at running his estates. Those who did not like the brash young Henry V inevitably pinned their hopes on the steady March.

Brambridge House lies off the B3335 north of Southampton. The haunting here is something of a mystery.

The field in front of Brambridge House where the ghostly cavalrymen have been seen.

British light dragoons of the Napoleonic Wars in action in Spain. The descriptions of the ghostly horsemen of Brambridge House seem to match these uniforms and may indicate an origin for the otherwise mysterious haunting.

March knew that usurpation was a dangerous game and preferred to stay loyally on his estates. Others were more daring and they cooked up a plot to murder Henry in Southampton and put March on the throne. The conspiracy was helped by a healthy chest full of French gold delivered to Lord Henry Scrope of Masham. At the last minute the conspirators decided to widen their plot to include men in positions of authority who were known to be hostile to Henry. One of these was Sir John Oldcastle, who disagreed with Henry's intolerance toward men who criticised the Pope's rule over the Church. Oldcastle was both astonished and appalled. Whatever his quarrels with Henry he would not agree to his murder. Oldcastle betrayed the plot to the King.

Henry at once summoned a trial of the leading conspirators by their peers, and a panel of Lords met in the main room of the Red Lion, a chamber now called the Courtroom. There, three noblemen were tried and sentenced to death in a single day: Lord Scrope, Richard Earl of Cambridge and Sir Thomas Grey. At dusk the three condemned men were marched out under armed guard to the Bargate where they were beheaded.

King Henry went on to invade France and win the glorious victory of Agincourt. The condemned men, meanwhile, have returned periodically to the Red Lion as ghosts. Their phantoms emerge with bowed heads from the front door and shuffle off toward Bargate. They have been seen numerous times, their identity being confirmed by their clothes.

There is a mystery at Brambridge, north-east of Southampton on the B3335, where the road runs past what was once the main entrance to Brambridge House. The gateway is now closed off by barbed wire and tangled undergrowth blocks the way. However, the towering lime trees that form a magnificent double avenue leading from the main road to the house still stand as impressive as ever. They were planted in around 1805 when pollarded limes were in great demand to provide timber for musket stocks. When the Napoleonic Wars ended at Waterloo in 1815, the limes were not by then mature, so they were never harvested. They stand today as tall and impressive as any trees in Hampshire and are a well-known local landmark.

The ghosts, and the mystery, belong to the wide grassy field to the north of the magnificent avenue. The field is used to graze horses and other livestock, though it is sometimes empty. It is a generally peaceful and rural scene. But it was very far from peaceful late one evening not so very long ago.

A lady living in Winchester was driving home with her husband from visiting friends for dinner in Eastleigh. As she passed the avenue of trees heading north, her husband said, 'Look. There in that field. Something is going on.'

The lady looked and was surprised to view a scene of confusion and mayhem. In the bright moonlight bathing the field she saw men riding horses, while other men were running around on foot. The men on horseback had long jackets that fell down over their hips and the horses' flanks. The men on foot also wore coats. This was odd as it was a warm summer's evening. Within seconds the car was past the field. She came to a halt.

'We had better go back,' she told her husband. 'It might be vandals chasing the horses or poachers.' He agreed and she backed her car up.

The field was completely empty and peaceful. There was nothing in sight. She and her husband compared notes. They had both clearly seen men on foot running around and horses rearing and careering around as if frightened. Her husband had seen a man on a horse with his arm raised and wearing a long coat that came down over the horses' sides. He thought perhaps he had his arm raised to hit somebody and may have been holding something in it. He thought the men were fighting, but she was not sure about this. And now there was nothing there except the wind and the trees.

Responding to the lady's request for information, I came to Brambridge one chilly winter's afternoon. There was the field and the avenue of trees, but no ghosts. A man pulled up in a Land Rover and started unloading horse feed to take to the horses in the field. Did he know anything about the strange apparition?

'Can't say I do,' he replied. He looked around the field. 'Mind you the big house has been used for all sorts of things. Back in the Napoleonic Wars it was used to house French prisoners of war. And it has had plenty of famous people stay there. That might have something to do with it.'

I decided to undertake some research. It transpired that Brambridge had, indeed, had some famous residents. Chief among these was young Maria Smythe, daughter of the owner Walter Smythe. Maria is far better known by her widowed name of Mrs Fitzherbert. She married King George IV when he was Prince of Wales, albeit illegally. Records confirm that the house was rented out during the Napoleonic Wars.

If it had been a camp for prisoners, it would have been surrounded by wooden huts housing the prisoners. The open field now grazed by horses would have been an ideal setting. Any trouble here, and there was certainly trouble at other such camps, would have been put down by the local yeomanry or by soldiers stationed nearby. The costumes described as being worn by the horsemen of the apparition were similar to those worn by dragoons and yeomanry at the time.

The dining area at the White Horse near Romsey. The white lady has been seen recently in this area of the pub.

The Palmerston Restaurant in Romsey where the upper floors are haunted by a ghost nicknamed 'Charlie'.

Was the mysterious ghostly scene glimpsed by moonlight a recreation of a riot or uprising by the French prisoners of war, or was it something quite different? We shall probably never know.

'Oh, you'll want to talk to Margaret,' said Joe the manager when I introduced myself at the White Horse pub on the A3090 east of Romsey, just before the road enters the village of Ampfield. 'She has worked here for years. She knows all about our lady ghost.'

I settled back into my chair beside the glowing log fire which dominates the front bar of the pub, and sipped my cider while I cast my eye over the menu while waiting for Margaret to arrive. After a few minutes the waitress bustled up.

'You've come about our lady ghost, then,' said Margaret. 'I'll tell you all about her.'

It seems that this particular ghost does not like to be left alone. In fact, she is rather prone to following people about, which can be very unnerving. The previous landlord and landlady, Theresa and Alan, had a fair amount of trouble with the ghost. She appeared most often in the private flat upstairs. First came a vague feeling that you were not alone, then a very definite sense that you were being followed. Sometimes the feeling faded away, but sometimes the feeling would become quite overpowering. And then the ghost appeared.

This particular phantom seems to be of a Victorian lady, dressed in a white or cream dress which reaches to the floor and has full-length sleeves. She rarely remains visible for very long before fading away.

'We had a spot of bother with one of our barmaids a little while back,' confided Margaret. 'While we were clearing up one night after last orders this girl got a funny feeling like someone was watching her. Then she walked out to her car round the back and got convinced that she was being followed. So she called the police on her mobile phone. Of course, I think it was just our lady in white up to her usual tricks.'

I asked Margaret if she had ever seen the ghost herself?

'Not seen her, no. But I have felt her. Come with me.' I followed Margaret through a doorway and past the side bar towards the back of the pub. There was a spacious restaurant area where the tables were laid for meals. Margaret pointed to a table set against the wall.

I was clearing up in here after one lunchtime when I felt the lady was about. You know, like somebody was following me about. Doesn't normally bother me I've worked here so long. Anyway, as I was clearing this table I felt a tap on my back. Like two taps as if someone wanted my attention. Well, I turned round but of course there was nobody there. Then Theresa came through the door from the upstairs flat. She looked at me and says 'Why whatever is the matter'. So I tell her that somebody was tapping me on the back and I wanted them to leave off doing it.

I looked around the pub. It certainly was a very atmospheric place, though it was more welcoming than anything else.

Now that fireplace you were sitting next to, that's a funny thing too. Many's the night I'd sit up there with Theresa and Alan after we'd shut up for the night. We'd be toasting crumpets on the log fire, then smother them with butter before scoffing them up.

And some nights there'd be these noises. Well, sounds like. Like there was somebody crawling over the floor, but the noises were coming from up the chimney. Now here's the funny bit. If you went round the back to the other fireplace and listened there, you could not hear a thing. But the chimneys join up just a little way up the flue. Funny that. These strange sounds like somebody crawling about up one chimney, but not up the other.

DRAGGING AN UNOCCUPIED DOG-COLLAR behind him, this constable strode majestically to the lock-up unaware that the arrested dog had " sloped."

An incident involving a Romsey copper that dates to about the time of the phantom policeman. Certainly the ghost wears a uniform of this 1920s vintage.

From the White Horse I moved on into Romsey itself. The weather had turned into a miserable and wet day by the time I arrived. Rain drizzled down from the grey skies in a constant stream of dampness that got everywhere. It was not, on the whole, a nice day.

So it was just as well that a warm welcome waited at the Palmerston Restaurant on the Market Square. The reason for the visit lurked upstairs where the public do not go but where, much to their displeasure, the staff do have to venture from time to time. For the attic and the top floor are the home to a grey-haired old man who goes by the name of Charlie. Nobody knows if that is his real name, for the origins of the ghost are obscure, but that is what the staff call him, so that is good enough for me.

Sometimes Charlie just sits about upstairs. He can startle those who thought they were alone, but otherwise he just sits there. But he can take on a more mischievous mood as well. His favourite trick is to switch the lights on or off. More than once the manageress has switched off all the lights and locked up, only to look back and see the light on in the upstairs room where Charlie is most often seen. Members of staff looking for stores upstairs can find themselves suddenly plunged into total darkness. Very unnerving.

Just as inexplicable, but less menacing, is Charlie's fascination with the toilet. It has been known to flush when nobody is in the room at the time. He also has a liking for doors, usually the ones that can be slammed shut with a loud crash when people have their backs turned. There are times when Charlie seems definitely to resent the intrusion of the living into his home upstairs. There can be a feeling of very clear tension upstairs. It is never as strong as outright hostility, but there is a real feeling that whoever is there would rather be left alone. A small shove in the back can encourage the person upstairs to leave. It usually works.

I made my notes about Charlie's activities with interest. Duty done, I turned to face the elements raging outside. The steady drizzle had escalated to a regular downpour, and the wind was lashing the rain across the slick pavements. It did not look at all inviting. Even the poor old statue of Lord Palmerston looked thoroughly fed up. This was not like the great

The ghostly Roundhead of Romsey as described to the author by an eyewitness.

nineteenth-century politician who had been MP for Romsey. He was better known for his firebrand speeches and sense of humour. It was Palmerston who sent gunboats off to solve disputes in remote corners of the empire, and he who led Britain through the Crimean War against Russia, famous for the Charge of the Light Brigade.

And there I was looking at a fine statue of this statesman streaming with rain and buffeted by the wind. By contrast, the restaurant was warm and cosy, and there were now some empty chairs as the lunchtime crowd thinned out. But no! I had another ghost to investigate and fortunately it was just on the other side of the square.

August 1642 was, on the whole, a good month for Romsey. But one late August day was a very bad day in Romsey for the two men who rode into town that summer evening. Their misfortune was to lead to Romsey's most disturbing haunting.

These were troubled times for England, as the spring and summer of 1642 saw the kingdom slip into a Civil War between the Royalist Cavaliers and Parliamentary Roundheads. Hampshire was staunchly Royalist and the people of Romsey were no exception. They were most displeased, therefore, when the Parliamentarian Sir Thomas Fairfax turned up in July with a strong force of armed men.

Fairfax had come to negotiate with the city fathers of Portsmouth, then a fortified town. The Royalist mayor of Portsmouth would not let Fairfax in, so the Parliamentarian commander lodged at The Swan Inn in Romsey. By mid-August Fairfax gave up trying to talk Portsmouth out of its loyalty to the King. He rode off with his men, much to the relief of Romsey.

Then news arrived in the town that King Charles had raised the Royal Standard in Nottingham and was calling on all loyal men to serve under his banner and crush the treason and rebellion of Parliamentary men, such as Fairfax. Romsey rejoiced.

So it was unfortunate that two of Fairfax's troopers chose that moment to ride into town. It is not recorded why they came. Perhaps Fairfax had sent them back on some mission; perhaps they had been away and were returning to where they thought their commander would be. We do not know.

What we do know is that the men of Romsey had been drinking and were in a vengeful mood. The two troopers were grabbed and torn from their horses. Ropes were strung over the iron bracket which held the sign of the Swan Inn and the troopers strung up. The hanging was not done skilfully and the poor men took some time to die.

It is this grisly event that led to the haunting. Over the years many people out late at night have come across the phantom of one of these Roundhead troopers. The ghost seems to be seen most often around the Conservative Club, formerly the Swan Inn, but is also seen around the corner near the abbey.

One witness described the apparition to me in some detail:

It was late on a Saturday night. I had been to a friend's house and was walking home. As I came round the corner [from the abbey into the square] I saw this chap outside the Club. I thought they must have been having a fancy dress party or something as he was dressed in armour. He just stood there, not moving. Like he was lost or something. As I got closer, he turned round. I thought he was going to ask to borrow my mobile to call a taxi. But he just looked right through me like I was not there. He put his hand to his throat and then just vanished. It was like puff and he was gone. I'd had a few myself that night, but I know what I saw.

The man then drew a sketch of the ghost. I have tidied it up a bit, and it is reproduced here.

I am not one to pour cold water on such stories, but the sketch is odd. It shows a Roundhead trooper well enough, but like they are illustrated in books. In August 1642 the war had scarcely begun and troops on either side were not well equipped. If this is the Romsey ghost, he is remarkably well kitted-out for a trooper of the date.

Never mind. After all, many other people have seen or heard the Roundhead troopers of Romsey. Some people have reported that the ghost staggers about clutching its throat and making the most dreadful gurgling and gasping noises, as if being choked to death. Most who have seen it say it is a very unpleasant and startling sight. There can be little doubt that something is seen hovering around the Conservative Club, once headquarters to Fairfax and his men.

Rather less disturbing is the phantom copper of Romsey. The rain had eased off by the time I left the Conservative Club to seek out his haunts. I had been put on to this ghost by a Mrs M (she would rather not have her name in print). 'He was stood there as clear as day,' Mrs M had told me. 'Just like you. Solid. In books and on films you see ghosts floating above the ground or going all see-through. He was not like that at all. He was solid and real. He was really there. Well, until he vanished that is.'

As I well know, this is typical of ghosts. Forget what you see and hear about fictional ghosts, the actual things seem very real indeed. Like Mrs M, many people who see a ghost do not realise, at first, what it is they are seeing. 'I thought it was someone in fancy dress', is a typical comment. And yet there is usually something odd about the ghost, something that is strangely out of place, though it is difficult for the witness to put their finger on it. It is as if you are looking at a painting where the perspective has been painted incorrectly. Everything looks right enough, but there is something very definitely wrong.

Back to Mrs M and her ghost. She had seen the phantom copper of Romsey. This ghost is not so well known as the Roundhead trooper, nor does he seem to be seen so often. He is, however, rather more mobile. I know of two places where he has been seen: Winchester Road by Cupernham Lane, and on the Broadwater Road. There may be more locations, for other accounts that I have traced do not pinpoint the location of the sighting.

So who is he? Well, according to Mrs M's account he wears the uniform of days gone by, but not too far back in history. Another person to see the ghost, Mrs Perry, saw the phantom copper on the Winchester Road and gave a more detailed description. Judging by these, I reckon the ghost dates from the period between the world wars. He wears a wool serge uniform with what appears to be a cape slung back off his shoulder, and a good solid helmet tops his head. Whenever he is seen the phantom copper just stands there. He does not walk as if on patrol, nor does he seem to be taking much notice of what goes on around him. He just stands and stares.

Given that the spectre is a policeman of the 1920s or 1930s, I set out to try to track him down. The only record I could find of the Romsey Police making the national news in that period came in 1923. And it was altogether too silly to account for the haunting. There had been a series of attacks on children by a dog running loose. As a result a by-law was passed that all dogs had to be kept on leashes by their owners. Any loose dog would be rounded up and, if found to be guilty of the attacks, would be put down.

In October one of Romsey's finest found a loose dog and promptly grabbed it. To be honest, the little Airedale terrier did not look much like the fearsome beast reported by the children, but orders were orders. The dog had to be taken in for identification. The policeman slipped a collar on the hound and set off back to the police station in The Hundred, leading the terrier behind him.

A contemporary newspaper takes up the tale:

> Then the dog began to follow the policeman as he led the way towards the station-house. The small crowd which had gathered to witness the occurrence grew, as small crowds will, into a fairly large one. Despite the smiles of the populace, the dignity of the law had to be upheld; but when the smiles of the crowd which followed became audible in the form of tittering, the constable looked round to see the cause. The cause was plain. The dog had become tired of the policeman's company and had broken arrest. He had slipped his head out of the collar and the policeman was merely dragging the empty collar along the ground by the string. The tittering grew into a laugh when the crowd found the policeman had discovered the situation, but the law had a card up its sleeve. The policeman solemnly conveyed the collar to the police-station in lieu of its wearer as evidence of arrest.

Embarrassing, no doubt, but enough to cause the poor policeman to return in spectral form? I doubt it. Rather more promising as a candidate is the unfortunate policeman who was run down and killed by a car on the Winchester Road. At least, so it is said. When I called at the police station nobody knew anything about this accident. Perhaps it was too long ago for the force to recall it. But the ghost remembers.

Hinton Ampner Gardens are located off the A272, a few miles east of Winchester and are well signposted. They are open at weekends and on some weekdays during the summer months. The hauntings at Hinton Ampner were so famous, so dramatic and the witnesses so impeccable that the strange events became known simply as The Great Haunting. Even today, two centuries after the supernatural events reached a terrifying climax, the phantoms remain.

I came to Hinton Ampner just after the gardens opened for the spring and summer seasons. Vast swathes of bulbs nodded their heads in a gentle spring breeze as a warm sun bathed the Hampshire countryside. In my pocket I had a fading, yellowing pamphlet written some years previously that gave a first-hand account of the supernatural events that once plagued this beautiful spot.

The Great Haunting of Hinton Ampner began soon after the death of the 4th Baron Stawell on 2 April 1755. It was, at first, a fairly conventional haunting of the type that I have found and investigated in many places. The ghost of Lord Stawell was seen wearing a brown suit of country clothes, walking through the house. He was seen most often in, or near, the Yellow Bedchamber which had been his old bedroom.

When he died Stawell left an only daughter, Mary, who had married the Rt Hon. Henry Bilson-Legge. The Bilson-Legges were happy in their London home, rarely visiting Hinton Ampner. Their reluctance to use the house may have been triggered by the fact that the local villages were awash with gossip about Lord Stawell's later years. Mary's mother – another Mary – had died in 1740. Her younger sister, Honoria, had by then moved into the house and, to the scandal of the county, she stayed there after her sister passed away. It was widely rumoured that Honoria and Lord Stawell were lovers, and generally believed that a baby had been born but had soon died. Certainly a carpenter had been called in to construct a small, hidden chamber beneath the floorboards of the dining room. Honoria had died in 1754, a year before her supposed lover.

In 1765 the Bilson-Legges rented the property out to a Mr and Mrs Ricketts. The Ricketts brought with them their servants from London and kept on only the local outdoor staff. Within

The gateway to Hinton Ampner Gardens, off the A272. The placid scene and tranquil gardens give no hint of the terrifying haunting that took place here some years ago.

weeks of moving in, the Ricketts' servants began to report a mysterious intruder to the house. From the description of a middle-aged man in a brown suit this was undoubtedly the ghost of Lord Stawell, who had never abandoned his hauntings. By the autumn of 1768, the phantom Lord Stawell had been joined by a second ghost. This was a lady in a heavy silk gown which rustled audibly as she hurried through the dining room and adjacent chambers.

Mrs Ricketts began keeping a journal of the strange phenomena plaguing her house. It records not just the two ghosts – seen about every six weeks or so – but also the sounds of footsteps. It was this booklet that I was reading as I wandered through the magnificent gardens.

It was on 2 April 1771, the anniversary of Lord Stawell's death, that things took a turn for the worse. As well as the ghosts, now being seen much more often, the doors of the house began to be thrown open, then slammed shut with great violence. Most disturbing to Mrs Ricketts, whose husband was away in the West Indies on business, were the voices. A man and a woman were heard muttering as if in conversation. Later, the voices were heard clearly arguing in the dining room, but only when the room was empty. They stopped abruptly if a person entered. On 5 May the male ghost entered Mrs Rickett's bedroom in what was clearly a bad temper. He glared at her, and hit the headboard with an audible thump.

The next day, Mrs Ricketts sent for her brother. The man was a no-nonsense sea captain named John Jervis, then aged thirty-six. Jervis already had a formidable reputation as a fighting captain in the wars against the French. He would later become an admiral and defeat a combined French, Spanish and Dutch fleet off Cape St Vincent. He ended his life as Earl St Vincent, having served as First Lord of the Admiralty, and was generally considered an honest and trustworthy soul.

At Hinton Ampner, Jervis not only saw the ghosts, but heard the ghostly argument that this time ended in a piercing shriek that awoke everyone in the house. After a week of phantom horrors, Jervis persuaded his sister to pack up her household and move out. Although the rent had been paid to the end of the year, the Ricketts never returned. It was the sensational accounts of the hauntings given at London parties by Mrs Ricketts and Captain Jervis that ensured the fame of the Great Haunting.

The Brushmaker's Arms at Upham are the scene of a long-lasting and active haunting linked to a murder.

The rear bar of the Brushmaker's Arms, where most of the more active haunting is reported to take place.

In January 1772 new tenants, the Lawrence family, moved in. They left suddenly, and no new tenants could be found, so Mr Bilson-Legge had the house pulled down. A small skull was found hidden in a wooden box beneath the dining room floorboards.

Bilson-Legge's daughter, Lord Stawell's granddaughter, built a new Hinton Ampner House and moved into her home in 1803. It is this house which forms the central feature of the Hinton Ampner Gardens, run today by the National Trust.

Although the most dramatic manifestations vanished with the demolition of the old house, there is still a ghost at Hinton Ampner. She now seems to be a gentle soul with none of the drama or malevolence of past years. Dressed in a long silk gown, she walks slowly around the site of the old house. Is she seeking something that she lost? Something small and hidden away in a wooden box to avoid scandal? Who knows?

The Brushmaker's Arms at Upham is easy enough to find, but actually visiting it requires a bit more dedication. The B2177 runs through Lower Upham. You need to turn north in the middle of the village along the lane signposted to Baybridge. This will lead you to Upham itself. The lane enters the village, then turns sharp right past the church. About 100 yards after this turn is a narrow side lane to the left. The Brushmaker's Arms is up this side turning. It is no good driving up the turning, however, as the lane is far too narrow to park on. Best to leave your car near the church and walk, though make sure you have not obstructed any of the driveways or private parking places with which the village abounds.

The effort is well worth it, for the Brushmaker's Arms is exactly the sort of friendly, jovial local pub that everyone would want to have at the end of their road. Apart from the murders, that is. Of course, both killings happened many years ago. Nobody has been murdered here for ages.

The less said about the gruesome events down in the cellar the better. They do not make for family reading and, in any case, have nothing to do with the haunting. It is the murder in the upstairs front bedroom that causes all the trouble and which brought me to this charming pub.

'I'll fetch Jill', said the barman when I called, and he trotted off upstairs.

'Here about the old feller upstairs?' asked a bearded man nursing a pint of ale at the bar. I confirmed that I was. 'Come to the right place for ghosts,' the man continued. He pointed out a framed certificate hanging on the wall by his head. It was from Teacher's Whisky and confirmed that the Brushmaker's Arms had come in the top twelve of the 'Most Haunted Pubs in Britain Contest' held in 1982. I asked the man if he had seen the ghost.

'No trouble there,' chipped in a man sitting at a table by the window. 'You're talking to our resident spirit right now.' He laughed. 'Been here long enough to qualify as a ghost yet?' he asked the bearded man.

'Only since I retired from the BBC,' came the reply. 'What's that, 15 years now? Not as long as Rob there.' He pointed at the other man at the table, a distinguished looking gent with silver hair. 'How long you been coming here, Rob.'

'Ooh. Must be near seventy years now,' declared Rob. 'Man and boy, I been coming here. Course back then they weren't too particular about how old a boy was. If you done your hard work on the farm, you got your beer. Very haunted this place, mind.'

'Yep,' continued his friend. 'Saw it myself in here. A few years back now. I was sitting at the bar, bout where you are, when the bottles started moving. They fell off the shelf, then flew across the bar. It was like someone was throwing them, but they didn't break. Just shot across the room and landed.'

It looked like the banter might go on for some time, but the landlady Jill arrived at that point to fill me in. The ghost is that of a sixteenth-century man named Mr Chickett. It was he who had the building constructed as part-house, part-brush factory — hence the pub's unique name. As the man grew older, his fortune grew greater. He would sit upstairs in his bedroom, counting out his gold and silver coins before stashing them away safely in a hidden compartment. It was not, however, hidden well enough. One morning his workers arrived to find old Mr Chickett battered to death, his room ransacked and his money stolen.

Ever since then, the ghost has walked. The most usual manifestation is the sound of footsteps which are heard in the bar directly underneath the room where the murder was committed. Less often the sound of chinking coins is heard from the same small room. Objects being moved around in the bar are a regular occurrence, although they are not actually seen to move very often. More usually an object is found in one place when it had been put in another.

The ghost himself is seen only rarely. Jill revealed:

Last time was about three years ago. I was upstairs doing some paperwork in the office. Suddenly I heard the door to the front bedroom [where the murder was committed] slam shut, very hard and loud. I looked round and there was the outline of a man, like a shadow on the wall, moving off. Only it couldn't be a shadow as the sun was not out. It was definitely a man moving down the corridor. Mind you, we haven't seen him since. People hear him of course. But I think he must like us. We get no trouble.

The landlord of the White Lion at Soberton, Graham Acres, was equally forthcoming about his ghost in a letter:

This is the story as I understand it. I am led to believe that the pub cellar was used as the mortuary until the turn of the 19th century — makes sense since it is cold and they buried them within a couple of days. I believe that the old road came across the down on a track known as the Driftway, across the front of the pub, down Church Meadow (lined with lime trees), forded the river and then via the riverside to Tichfield (then an important harbour). Bearing in mind horses could not pull carts up steep hills, this makes the current roads footpaths in those days.

It seems that 'Lucy' was a young maid in service of some description – probably in the big house – and managed to get run over and killed by a cart in front of the pub. They popped her downstairs, but when they came to bury her they discovered she was a Catholic. This was back in 1600 and something when that sort of thing was taken a lot more seriously. And there was no Catholic church round here. She was therefore buried in unconsecrated ground and has haunted the pub ever since.

I have had 3 people (who turned out to be mediums) ask me whether I was aware that there was a presence. Each one knew it was a young girl and each one told me that she was benign to me. Several other people have felt very cold and uncomfortable at a certain point in the bar. I have had 1 or 2 strange happenings, but the dog's hair only stood on end once.

Some versions of the story have it that Lucy was a dairymaid searching for her errant butler husband who used to sneak off to the pub for drinks. There are carvings on the village's church tower of man, woman, key and pail, which are said to be this pair who became rich and built the tower.

The fact that the lanes near Bramshott are haunted is not in doubt. Everyone that I spoke to was quite certain on that point. The dispute is over what exactly the lanes are haunted by. Bramshott lies just north of the A3 where it swoops round to the north of Liphook. To reach the village, and its surrounding lanes, take the B3004 north from Liphook. As soon as you have crossed the bridge over the A3, peel off to the right. This lane takes you down to Bramshott.

The man who brought me to this charming village was in no doubt at all. 'The ghost is that of a highwayman,' he asserted confidently. 'Or it might be a cavalier from the Civil War. Not sure really. But he definitely has a pistol and a big hat.'

The lanes near Bramshott are haunted by a quite remarkable phantom, though not even the locals can agree on what it is.

Had the ghost actually been seen I asked hoping for some details of dress which might sort the matter out.

'Oh yes, no doubt about that. Though I haven't actually seen it myself, mind you. It was my dad. He saw it. A big chap on a big horse wearing a big hat. Definitely a highwayman, though. Unless he was a cavalier, that is.'

In fact, the ghost could easily be both and each other at the same time. Until the 1640s the robbers who lurked on the roads of England to rob unwary travellers were a fairly unpleasant bunch of men who went by the name of footpads. 'Mugger' would be the modern word to describe such unsavoury characters. Then came the English Civil Wars and the social upheavals which accompanied the violence. Several Royalist gentlemen lost all their lands and wealth in the revolution. They did, however, retain their weapons, fine clothes and swift horses. Some went abroad to fight as mercenaries, but others stayed in England to rob travellers, then escape on their fast horses.

These men were very different from the violent footpads. They were gentlemen who displayed exquisite manners while engaged in highway robbery. Soon the highwayman had been born as a specific type of criminal. Dressed in top-quality clothing, he rode a beautiful horse and engaged in acts of gallantry while robbing his victims.

Captain John Hind was one such man ruined by the war who took to the road in a life of crime. He actually tried to rob Oliver Cromwell on one occasion. Claude Duval came later, and is famous for having once danced a quadrille with a pretty girl he found in a coach he was robbing.

He gave the girl back her jewels in thanks for the dance. Most of these men ended up swinging from a rope, of course, and a few were shot during highway robberies.

Was the Bramshott phantom such a man? I set off to investigate.

'Oh yes, the ghost,' replied an elderly lady I met in the village. 'I recall my grandmother telling me about it.'

Could the lady identify the ghost?

'Oh yes. It's a pig.' I tried to talk about a highwayman. But the lady soon made herself clear. 'A pig. You know. Four legs. Goes "oink". Mind you, not a real pig, see. It's a fairy pig. Nasty evil thing.' The lady looked over her shoulder. 'My grandmother did tell me that those as take it for a stray pig and go after it just end up getting themselves lost. It's a naughty fairy, see. It likes to get people lost. You follow it for ages. Then it shrinks and shrinks until it's no bigger than a cat. Then it vanishes and there you are. Lost.'

I thanked the lady and moved on.

Near the church, I met a young woman. She smiled and said, 'Oh yes, the haunted lanes. We all know about that. Don't believe it myself, of course, but my dad goes on about it sometimes.' What is the ghost?

A highwayman of the mid-eighteenth century. At least one witness has described the Bramshott ghost as looking like this sketch.

'Well, if you believe such things, it's a chap playing a flute or pipes or something.'

A highwayman playing music? Well perhaps, but no. 'Not on a horse, silly,' said the young woman. 'Just standing by the road playing his flute or whatever.'

It was by now coming on to drizzle. I did not fancy getting wet, so I retired to the handily nearby Green Dragon pub. 'Been out walking?' asked the barmaid. 'You want to watch yourself round here. Those lanes are haunted, you know. Dead scary, I'm told.' What are the lanes haunted by? 'Oh everyone knows that. My mum told me all about it. It's the ghost of an old lady.'

The ghost that resides on the B3047 near Alresford is more definite – it is an old, grey mare. I got a steer on this phantom from a Mr Annis from Upham. He said that twenty-five years ago he was driving through Alresford, as although he lived in Southampton, working at the hospital, his parents lived in Earlsfield. He did the drive a lot and knew the road well. He drove an old Morris Minor, with the flat windscreen and little wipers. It was dusk and it was drizzling. He had his wipers and lights on. As he went up the hill towards the pub and petrol station he suddenly saw a grey horse walk out into the road right in front of him. He slammed on his brakes and shuddered to a stop. He was convinced he had hit the horse on its hindquarter with his left wing. But the horse just carried on walking and vanished straight through the hedge – no gate or anything. It really shook him up. 'I can see it clearly even now. A grey dappled horse, quite small though. Like a pony.'

As I said when I began, the ghosts of Hampshire are a mixed lot. Horses and all.